Physical Development in the Early Years

Lynda Woodfie

continuum
LONDON • NEW YORK

Continuum International Publishing Group

The Tower Building
11 York Road
London SE1 7NX

15 East 26th Street
New York
NY 10010

www.continuumbooks.com

British Library Cataloguing-in-Publication Data
A catalogue record for this book is available from the British Library.

ISBN: 0–8264–6871–3 (paperback)

Typeset by BookEns Ltd, Royston, Herts.
Printed and bound in Great Britain by
Antony Rowe Ltd, Chippenham, Wiltshire

Physical Development in the Early Years

Other Classmates:

2nd Series
Successful Subject Co-ordination – Christine Farmery
Parent Partnership in the Early Years – Damien Fitzgerald
Playing Outdoors in the Early Years – Ros Garrick
Assemblies Made Easy – Victoria Kidwell
Homework – Victoria Kidwell
Getting Promoted – Tom Miller
ICT in the Early Years – Mark O'Hara
Creating Positive Classrooms – Mike Ollerton
Getting Organized – Angela Thody and Derek Bowden

1st Series
Lesson Planning – Graham Butt
Managing Your Classroom – Gererd Dixie
Teacher's Guide to Protecting Children – Janet Kay
Tips for Trips – Andy Leeder
Stress Busting – Michael Papworth
Every Minute Counts – Michael Papworth
Teaching Poetry – Fred Sedgwick
Running Your Tutor Group – Ian Startup
Involving Parents – Julian Stern
Marking and Assessment – Howard Tanner

Contents

Contents

Preface

This book covers the growth, physical development and *physical* education of the young child from birth to eight years. The interaction between the various physical and sensory systems is examined, and the journey of development and of learning undertaken by the child is outlined.

The aim of this book is to set out as a guiding principle a *typical* pathway of growth and development for a *typical* child. It can be seen that learning through and with the body is real learning. Many practical instances and examples are presented alongside the theoretical frameworks, and suggestions are given which show how development of whole body awareness, sensory integration, skill acquisition and enhancement can be facilitated by knowledgeable practitioners. The intention is to examine the complexities of this *typical* journey; particular motor difficulties and special educational needs are not addressed.

To avoid repetition of the rather ponderous 'he/she', or 's/he' forms, the child is referred to throughout as 'he', although it is obvious that both girls and boys are included in the comments. Where there is a need to provide gender emphasis and/or difference this is made clear, and in the real-

life examples the names of the individual children are used.

Similarly, the term 'practitioner' is employed, to cover the range of adults who work with young children in the various settings, and is referred to as 'she'. The word 'teacher' is not always appropriate and the term 'teaching' can often mean facilitating in this context. Parents are the first teachers and role models of the children. Effort has been made to select terms appropriately to match situations and settings.

A personal belief in the importance of experiential learning underpins all that is written here. This book is a result of personal experience and of many years spent working with children, early years practitioners and students in their initial teacher training. This experience has been honed by personal study of the body and human movement at the Laban Centre, practical teaching of movement and dance, and research projects with young children and their teachers.

It is important to consider *how* children learn in the physical domain before considering *what* they should explore and how educators should teach or present the learning opportunities. It is vital that trainee and newly qualified teachers are taught about the developmental, experiential aspects of learning if they are to understand *why* they are undertaking activities with children.

The physical steps, skills and developmental milestones will be outlined in simple terms, and suggestions will be made for appropriate experiences across areas of learning. However, physical motor skill

development cannot be matched neatly with chronological development and it is important that learning experiences are devised to fit the particular needs of each child.

Strategies for improving practitioners' observation skills will be suggested. Ideas will be given which can facilitate skill acquisition and sensory learning. Safety issues will be considered and shown to be part of good, every-day planning and practice. Health, nutrition, the home environment and the role of parents are all important factors which affect learning. It will be seen that physical development should not be studied in isolation from other areas and that all learning depends upon physical competence and motor skill facility, working together with perceptual and sensory awareness. Physical learning, competence and confidence can be seen to run throughout *all* the areas of learning in the *Curriculum Guidance for the Foundation Stage* (QCA/DfEE 2000). Children become successful operators and learners as they acquire physical skill competence and the concomitant personal confidence. They learn to move and they move in order to learn.

Practitioners need to have a basic knowledge of the stages of physical and sensory development and the complicated interplay between the various systems involved. This knowledge will help them to support areas of learning and experience and to plan activities which are 'developmentally appropriate' (NASPE 1992, in Buschner 1994) for the children in their care.

The importance of enjoyable, play-based activity as a foundation for learning for all children will be

stressed throughout this book. Sound strategies for teaching and learning, based upon developmental principles, plus planning which allows time for children to explore, consolidate and be creative can all be seen to be essential components of early education. These principles can help to demonstrate the dangers of a too rigid, formalized early years curriculum.

Acknowledgements

Children teach me such a lot, as I work with them, teach them, observe them, and play with them. This teaching process has always been there, throughout my training and work as a teacher, advisory teacher and lecturer, and it is ongoing. I would like to thank all of the children for illuminating my work and my studies.

I would also like to thank my husband and my mother for their support, colleagues at Sheffield Hallam University for their constructive comments and Andrew Caldicott for his help with computing.

It is very important to express my thanks to all the Early Years practitioners with whom I have worked over many years. They have all contributed to the writing of this book.

Introduction

> *What a piece of work is a man! How noble in reason! how infinite in faculty! in form, in moving, how express and admirable! in action how like an angel! in apprehension how like a god! the beauty of the world!*
> William Shakespeare (*c.* 1602) *Hamlet*,
> lines 323–31

The human child is a tiny learning machine. Growth, development, acquisition of physical skills, sensory awareness and learning seem to happen at an astonishing rate.

The human child is indeed a formidable 'piece of work'!

However, the child is in the position of first-time learning: he is learning how to stand up and how to walk for the very first time. Engagement with the widening frontiers of his world is a massive undertaking. Physical development, growth and strength are manifested in increasing mastery of movement, negotiation and manipulation of the environment and the objects and people within it.

Adults do not remember going through these learning experiences and take for granted movement, manipulative skill and the functioning of all the senses and sensory systems. They have

mastery of many complex movement patterns without realizing it. An adult can walk across the room, drink a cup of tea, tie his shoelaces, and go up and down stairs quickly, without looking down. The adult just 'knows' where his mouth is in relation to the cup; he knows where the next stair is and how shoelaces behave. He does not need to employ *conscious* thought to do these things. The young child, in his position as first-time learner, does not just 'know'. He has to learn. Some of this learning seems to be almost pre-programmed into the child, with the learning seeming to happen at certain stages of life. Other aspects of learning take time, repetition and considerable effort. Some skills seem to be very difficult and progress is not always smooth.

However, as movement facility, manipulative skill and understanding improve, some aspects of learning seem to become second nature – almost automatic. The first steps taken by the child seem to take real effort, co-ordination and balance. Several months later, he walks and runs smoothly, without conscious effort or thought. The child now 'knows' how to walk; he has mastery of this motor skill. He also learns how to talk and, in a magical, mysterious way, 'knows' what red is.

This special kind of learning, this 'knowing' (Wittgenstein 1991, p. 3e), is an important area of study for all practitioners working with young children. It is necessary to study the physical development and the sensory/perceptual develop-ment stages and interactions which lead to this 'knowing'. What is not obvious to an onlooker, or to

the learner, is that another vital function is active: the human brain and nervous system. The brain, the spinal cord and nerve networks which make up the central nervous system govern all aspects of growth and neurological, muscular and emotional functioning. The brain can be said to control movement, even *unconscious*, automatic movement. Movement learning is a vital part of *all learning*. Perceptual development is also a vital part: the child who has learnt what red is has taken a great intellectual and cognitive step.

This child, this learning machine, is learning, growing and developing on all fronts – physical, emotional, social, linguistic, intellectual and creative. The whole child is developing, growing, learning, interacting and understanding his expanding world and how to be a successful operator within it.

1

Physical Development

This chapter will set out some developmental steps in basic language, so that a simple framework of growth steps and changes can be established. At the same time, it is important to note that growth and physical developmental steps do not all occur at set, programmed ages and in accordance with set timetables. Each child is an individual, and genetic, nutritional and environmental aspects are influential. Progress is made at different speeds and rates; there can be plateaux and retrograde steps. Development can be seen as a road along which *all* children travel, yet they do not all travel and make progress at the same speed and some children may pause at times and/or take detours along the way.

The whole child

The term 'physical development' provides several difficulties and complexities as one attempts to unravel it. 'Physical' sounds simple, relating to the body, and 'development' implies progress which is linear and incremental: it sounds a deceptively simple area for study.

However, as has been outlined in the Introduction, the physical being and physical growth cannot be

4

separated from the emotional, social, psychological whole person. Physical growth and development cannot be sectioned off and viewed as forming one particular entity; basic body management, control and competence affect confidence and all interaction with the environment and with other people. This means that the physical aspects of learning cannot be placed in one curricular 'box'.

Furthermore, although human growth and developmental stages and steps *do* follow a sequential pattern, the physical changes and progress of the human child cannot be simplistically related to age (Gallahue and Ozmun 1998). Where one child may walk at ten months, another may not walk until over sixteen months old.

Nevertheless, it is helpful for practitioners to have a concept of the basic growth patterns and developmental steps that occur, along with an approximate chronology. These milestones can provide useful knowledge as a baseline guide or yardstick so that practitioners can plan learning experiences for children which are appropriate and which match developmental levels.

Practitioners also need to know how physical skills are acquired and developed in order to break down skills into appropriate, attainable sub-skills and plan the next learning step. This understanding of how the body develops and acquires motor competence is vital so that practitioners do not present children with movement and manipulative tasks which are impossibly difficult and inappropriate for their developmental level. Similarly, children should not be under-challenged.

Physical Development in the Early Years

Practitioners can also view progress or delay against broad 'norms' (Sheridan 1995) and some motor difficulties may thus be identified in certain cases where children fail to meet the expected milestones. Experienced practitioners will know when to allay fears of parents regarding a child's difficulties or when to recommend consulting appropriate medical professionals.

A sound knowledge of these developmental milestones and the patterns of growth will form an underpinning framework for practitioners as they gain experience in practical work with children.

Patterns of growth

The neonate, or new-born, arrives in the world as an active learner, ready to survive and to begin functioning in the world outside the womb. The baby is dependent upon an adult for food and care. The length of a new-born baby is approximately half a metre and the baby's head is large, roughly a quarter of the length of the body. The bones of the skull are comparatively soft and flexible and there is incomplete fusion of the skull at the top of the baby's head (the *anterior fontanelle*) which can aid passage through the birth canal. In the first months of life the baby grows in length and weight and the brain and sensory systems develop rapidly (Keenan 2002).

Some basic and invariable patterns are present in maturation and growth in infants, as can be seen in *cephalocaudal* and *proximodistal* development.

In cephalocaudal (meaning literally, development, 'head to tail') maturation and growth occur in a head

to toe direction. In the womb, the head and major organs develop before the limbs and extremities. After birth the head of the infant is large and the brain is relatively developed; gradually the body grows and develops in strength, then later, the limbs. Similarly, in movement terms, the child first gains control in lifting up his head, then gradually he develops the strength to sit. After sitting, the child begins to develop the skills and strength to crawl. A head–body–limbs pattern of strength and mastery can be seen.

In proximodistal (meaning literally, development, 'from near to far') the maturational changes, growth and strength occur from the centre of the body outwards. Cell, nerve and organ development is more complete in the centre of the body, the trunk, before the extremities. The infant acquires control (as a result of growth and increased strength) in the neck and centre of the body before control develops in the fingers and the toes (extremities).

Growth spurts

Rapid spurts of growth occur in infancy and in puberty. During the middle childhood period, from seven to ten years approximately, growth is more steady. The chubby infant physique, with its very large head, changes through the toddler years. The body and limbs elongate after the third year, through into early and mid-childhood. The child will become taller and the head will not appear so large in comparison with the rest of the body. This is because the bones and muscles in the legs have grown in length and strength.

Milestones of development and movement

The following sections show broad, age-related expectations for the developing child. As already stressed, all children make individual progress and take individual steps along this road. As well as genetic makeup (plus patterns of physical growth and sensory maturation), the environment in which the child is living and growing affects development.

The new-born baby

Cameo

Baby Henry is one week old. His proud parents have already realized that Henry can wriggle and move and make his requirements known. He has differing types of cry which can indicate different needs, for example, when he wakes, if he is hungry or if he is uncomfortable or wet. He can curl his fingers around his father's finger. He can wave his arms and legs. Henry seems to know when his parents come into the room and when his mother is holding him he can gaze into her face. He seems able to copy facial expressions and appears to smile. He opens his mouth when his cheek is touched. He is already making his presence felt in this new world, with two adults at his beck and call!

The new-born baby is not an entirely passive, helpless being, as Henry's cameo shows. The new baby is an active learner as he experiences his environment through a range of senses. Some of the things Henry does are in reality reflex actions, which can be misinterpreted by parents as examples of precocious development. These reflex actions are inherent survival actions and are also the precursors to planned, voluntary movements. Several automatic reflex actions are present in the new-born baby, some of which disappear in the first weeks and months and others which remain throughout life. When a baby is touched on the cheek he will turn towards the touch to feed: this is the rooting, sucking reflex and is an example of a reflex action which disappears. The eye blink reflex (when an object approaches the eye, it reflexively blinks) is an example of a reflex action which is present at three months and remains throughout life (Cratty 1986).

Reflex actions cannot be controlled, they just happen. The new baby will show several touch response reflexes (rooting, sucking, grasping) and will show a startle reflex to sudden, loud noise. The rooting and sucking reflex actions occur when the baby is placed close to the mother's breast. The grasp reflex occurs when an adult finger is placed on the baby's palm and the baby's fingers close and grip.

Movement *self-righting* and muscle tone reflexes are present: if the baby is placed on his back and the head is turned, the trunk will turn towards the side that the head is facing; if the hips are turned one way the head will turn towards the same direction. These neck and body righting

reflexes can be said to be the body attempting to keep itself the *right* way up, a survival reflex action. New-born babies also exhibit reflexive breath holding and can 'swim' underwater, although not many parents would wish to test this reflex! These early reflexes are thought to be life-saving mechanisms (Cratty *ibid.*).

In the first weeks the baby can hear and 'see' close objects and can mirror facial expressions. He 'speaks' by crying and making some soft grunting sounds. He will sleep for many hours of the day. The new-born baby cannot lift up his head, roll over, reach or sit up. His muscles do not yet have anti-gravity strength.

In the first weeks and months

Some of the reflex actions disappear during the first weeks of life. The baby's head needs to be supported at all times, but, around the second month, the baby develops the labyrinthine righting reflex where there is the tendency and strength in the neck to lift the head upright against gravity even if the body is angled downward. This can be seen as a precursor to balance. If a baby exhibits a 'floppy' head at this stage it can be an indication of neurological problems and later movement difficulties. Similarly, excessive rigidity of tone of muscles (spasm) can indicate motor/movement and neurological problems. Health visitors and other medical practitioners are alert to these indications. Throughout life, extremes of poor muscle tone and rigidity continue to be possible indicators of motor problems (Cocks 1992).

In the first few weeks and months, if the baby is held out above the ground he will move his limbs in reflex actions of stepping, walking, crawling, climbing and swimming movements. He cannot *really* walk, crawl or swim, but these actions seem to be programmed into the baby.

Cratty (1986, p. 112) suggests that 'the presence of these interesting reflexes indicates how deeply locomotor activities are ingrained within the human nervous system.' This walking in the air disappears after three weeks of age and actual, real walking does not occur until between nine and eighteen months. The baby also carries out spontaneous movement: he will kick his legs, bounce, wave and flap his arms, and close his fingers. These movements are the baby's spontaneous exercise and rehearsals for real movement and show that the human body is made to move, to be dynamic.

Between three and six months

The baby is much stronger and more alert. He can track objects with his eyes. Muscle strength against gravity is increasing and the baby seems to strive to hold up his head. Between four and six months he can turn over, reach for objects and hold them, using a palmar grasp which is not a reflex. He can sit if supported. He may have some first teeth by now. His 'exercising' continues and he seems to enjoy moving and kicking. In order to develop true movement (lifting limbs) and to achieve stability (holding stillness) and balance he has to defeat gravity.

Physical Development in the Early Years

Between seven months and one year

Between seven and nine months the muscle strength needed to overcome gravity is increasing. This means having strength to lift parts of the body from the ground. The child is by no means supine any longer. He begins to creep, crawl and shuffle around the space at increasing speeds and can sit unsupported. He has increased trunk and limb strength and can pull himself up to a standing position by holding furniture. He will also begin to walk, again using furniture or parental assistance as support. Balance skill and strength are only just beginning to develop and he will fall back down onto his bottom if support is released. Crawling and walking are very important landmark skills as both involve oppositional movement (left hand, right leg; right hand, left leg) – what Dennison and Dennison (1994, p. 3) call 'bilateral movement skills'.

During this period the child begins to hold objects with finger and thumb. This is known as the pincer grasp or grip, and is much more sophisticated in sensory-motor terms than the reflex grasp of the new-born baby or the palmar grasp, as it indicates the first development of fine motor skills as well as a will to hold, examine and explore. The child will lean forward to reach objects and toys, and objects for exploration are frequently placed in the mouth.

At around twelve months old the child will show the beginnings of walking unaided.

Cameo

Bethan is thirteen months old. To the delight of her parents she has taken her first steps unaided. When she walks across the room Bethan appears to be really concentrating. She leans forward and lifts each leg quite high. She steps down with each foot in a purposeful manner. Her balance is precarious. She walks between furniture supports and sometimes she loses her balance and sits down rather abruptly onto her bottom. At other times she seems to be overcome by her own success and momentum and hurries on to the next piece of furniture. If her parents hold her hands her balance seems to be improved and if the other parent waits with arms outstretched Bethan can hurry across the space. She can manage to cross increasing areas of the room unaided and can be seen to sway and catch her balance at times. At other times she tips forward onto her hands. Bethan enjoys the activity and the praise of her parents.

Bethan has reached a major movement milestone and she shows some of the features and the difficulties of early walking. The skill of walking, in terms of motor skill and co-ordination, is very complicated and involves balancing, going off balance and then recapturing balance, the child adjusting stability all the time. Becoming vertical, standing and

walking require a shift in the centre of gravity (Bee 1995) and unaided walking requires time for the skill to become consolidated. The movements are slow and exaggerated. Speed and balance improve in the next few months.

Between one year and eighteen months

Skills in standing supported and in beginning to walk are now becoming more efficient. By sixteen months most children can walk short distances and can crawl up steps. As balance improves, the walking may be stopped by the child himself, by losing balance backwards or forwards in a premeditated fashion rather than simply falling onto his bottom. The child can manipulate toys, passing them from one hand to the other and holding with one hand and feeling with the other (Thelen 1995). He can drop toys and track them visually on the floor. The child enjoys using sounds and beginning language, knows his own name and can respond to it and to some words.

Up to and around two years

The child becomes much more inquisitive, and confidence in movement skill is increasing. The child enjoys movement and explores new ways to travel in space, around, over and under furniture and up steps and stairs. He still takes time to establish his balance. The child will climb stairs by putting one foot then the other on the same step. He may come down by sitting down on each stair or he may descend backwards, again putting both feet onto the step.

Between two and three years of age the child begins to travel with speed, almost running. He will jump from one step onto the ground with two feet. He may be able to use his hands to send a ball up in the air and will also try to direct a ball with his feet. He may have the manipulative skill, control and co-ordination to be able to stack a small tower of bricks. He can also scribble on paper using the hand he favours. Independent eating and drinking skills are improving and all of his first teeth may be through. The child is developing control over bowel movements. Between two and three years of age the child becomes aware that he is a boy, not a girl. This is known as developing gender identity (Smith *et al.* 2003, p. 187). At this stage the child can show signs of will and determination and will not understand sharing. He will play *near* other children, but not play *with* them. This is often referred to as 'parallel play' (Parten 1933, quoted in Curtis and O'Hagan 2003, p. 117).

Between three to five years

The child becomes more proficient in basic travelling and manipulating. Speed of movement, co-ordination and reaction are all improving as the child exhibits immature running, a kind of hurried trotting, at around three years of age, which lacks the true period of suspension from one leg to the other of mature running. He can jump from the ground and from a step, landing well on two feet, and he can stand on one leg for a short period of time, showing the beginnings of balance. He will enjoy hopping,

springing and bending down and looking through his legs at an upside down version of his world. Between these years the child will become more adventurous, enjoying climbing and experiencing swinging and being upside down (with appropriate adult support). He will become more confident at pushing and eventually riding on wheeled vehicles.

Both fine and gross motor skills develop as the child explores his world and the objects in it. Around four years of age the child begins to develop gender stability (Kohlberg 1966, in Harris and Butterworth 2002, p. 220); he can state the gender label of another person or a picture, but may become confused if, for example, a girl is dressed in boys' clothes.

The child's dressing skills improve with encouragement and he will be able to put on and take off some clothes and shoes, but will still need help with sleeves, buttons and fasteners and may continue to do so for the next few years. The ability to tie shoelaces successfully, for example, is one of the most complex motor and perceptual skill operations a human ever learns.

During this stage of development, confidence and enjoyment in moving and playing are evident. The child explores and experiments with a whole range of ways of moving and travelling, and running shows increasing elevation. Both fine and gross motor skills become more fluent and practised. Co-ordination improves rapidly and perceptual skills come into play as the child navigates around objects and furniture with increasing speed and agility. The child seems to be full of energy – kinetic energy, the energy to move.

Between the ages of three and five years there are increasing opportunities for exercise and acquisition of movement skills as the child meets new places, new people and new environments presented by the education system (playgroup, nursery, foundation/reception units, and infant school). These new adventures present emotional as well as physical challenges. It is not uncommon for the speech and movement skills of children to go back to toddler level at times of challenge and insecurity. The child seems to do this 'on purpose', and it is a very real plea for attention and security. It is essential for carers and practitioners to notice and praise achievement and to make sure that the new environment makes the child feel as secure as possible. Security will aid self-esteem and confidence, both of which are necessary for the child to take on new experiences, games and people. As these experiences are encountered, the perceptual and motor skills are exercised and enhanced. Meeting other children can mean that comparison and competition enter the arena.

Between six and eight years

Between six and eight years of age, the child is becoming used to a more formalized system of learning and to meeting differing challenges. At this stage the child has mastery of basic locomotive (travelling) and manipulative skills. Both fine and gross motor skills are developing and the child will show an inclination to practise and repeat moves. Left- or right-handedness is usually established by the age of six (Maude 2001, p. 11) and the dominance of one hand

over the other is important in motor skill terms: in effect the child develops bilateral skills, through which one hand can support while the dominant hand carries out more intricate operations. Before developing a favourite hand, the child may not cross the mid-line of the body to pick up items. Delay in developing hand dominance and bilateral skill can be an indicator for other motor skill problems. The child will also develop a favourite foot, and this usually matches the dominant hand (Maude *ibid.*). From the age of six years the child reaches the stage of gender constancy; he knows that gender remains consistent regardless of clothing, situation or time (Harris and Butterworth 2002, p. 220).

At this stage the child is taller and much stronger and can apply longer periods of concentration to tasks. Sending, receiving (precursors to catching, throwing and kicking) and object management skills are improving as the child becomes used to moving in space with other children and with an object (ball, bean bag, bat, rope). The child can listen to instructions and simple coaching points and carry them out. This is the period when practitioners should continue to provide task challenges and also introduce more directed skills teaching. It is the stage at which big differences in movement competence between children become evident, and the children themselves are very aware of this.

Summary

This chapter has outlined development in terms of the patterns of growth and the main movement and

Birth–first weeks	Reflex actions: rooting, grasping.
3–6 months	Strives to lift head, can turn over and sit supported.
6–8 months	Can sit unsupported, able to transfer objects from hand to hand.
8–12 months	Creeping, crawling, pulls up to stand, walks with help.
12–18 months	Walks unaided, climbs furniture, creeps backwards down steps.
2–3 years	Fine motor skills improving, explores travelling, climbs up and down stairs.
3–4 years	Can run and stop, tiptoe, come downstairs one step at a time.
4–5 years	Explores travelling and speeds, can hop, jump and ride a tricycle.
6–8 years	Explores range of travelling, balancing, fine motor tasks, games and equipment; sending and receiving develops into catching, throwing, kicking.

Table 1.1   Main movement milestones

developmental milestones from birth to eight years. For ease of reference these milestones are summarized in Table 1.1.

The importance of practitioners having a secure knowledge and understanding of these aspects is stressed in the SPEEL (Study of Pedagogical Effectiveness in Early Learning) Research Project Framework.

Overwhelmingly, early years managers/head-teachers and practitioners see knowledge of child development and, in particular, children's

learning as fundamental to effective teaching and learning.

Moyles *et al.* (2002, Introduction)

The beneficial aspects of good, appropriate practice form a two-way process: activities which match the developmental level of the child can consolidate and extend learning, whilst appropriate stimulation, interaction, action and challenge aid development. The child learns through engagement in movement and through his senses, and at the same time his movement and sensory skills are enhanced.

In an impoverished environment, lacking toys, space, adult attention and praise and adequate nutrition the child will fail to thrive and overall development and growth will be retarded. Movement is essential for healthy development and it is the medium for learning.

As the young child grows and gains in confidence and muscular strength he is very rarely still for long periods unless he is asleep. This world of action is a world for learning. The small baby's movements and sounds are his exercise systems and preparation for language. He explores the world through his senses. The young child, upright, mobile and active, continues this exploration. Play is his learning and exercise system: active play is the 'work-out' of the young child, this little learning machine.

2

Perceptual and Sensory-Motor Development

The developing and growing child interacts with the environment and the other humans, animals and objects around him within it. In order to do this all of the sensory systems are utilized. To operate and to move successfully, senses such as sight, touch, hearing, taste and smell, plus balance skills, judgements of space, force and weight all come into play and contribute to a consciousness of self and of one's self in this environment. Sorting, interpreting and making meaning from the information from the environment through the senses and through the body can be said to be perception. An account of physical development therefore cannot neglect consideration of perceptual and sensory-motor development.

The physical development of the body has been outlined. However, the major organ relating to all developmental progress and all physical processes is the brain. The human is not simply a moving, mechanical, physical body with a thinking brain in its head. The brain and body cannot be separated in this dualistic fashion. The brain and the central nervous system govern all other body systems and movement, and the study of neurological

functioning is a very complex science. Similarly, bodily well-being affects the functioning of the brain. This chapter aims to present a simplified view of perceptual and sensory-motor development. It can be helpful to utilize simple analogies and images as examples in order to present neurological and physiological aspects in an understandable manner.

Defining and understanding terms

Perceptual development: what does this mean?

A human being is not a robot. A robot can have a body which can be made to move following signals from its computer 'brain'. This computer-brain can even make the robot perform a type of speech and pick up or move objects. The robot, however, cannot taste, smell, feel happy, think, consider choices, hear, see or touch in the ways that a human can. The human is *aware*, he can *perceive* his environment through a range of senses and he can process this information; the human has emotions and feelings; the human can think. The human has consciousness; he knows he has a brain. The human knows he can think and consider. The human can think about thinking (meta-cognition). The robot cannot do this. It does not know it has a brain. The robot is not capable of true awareness or perception.

Perception is a complex process or ability. Closer consideration of the definition of perception shows

up this complexity. The *Chambers English Dictionary* (1990) states that to perceive is 'to become or be aware of through the senses: to get knowledge of by the mind: to see: to understand: to discern' and that perception is 'the act or power of perceiving: discernment: apprehension of any modification of consciousness: the combining of sensations into a recognition of an object.' Perception involves physical, mental and emotional processes. Making sense of the sensory information, sense of one's body and sense of the environment means that all these processes work and interact together before meaningful synthesis can occur: quite an achievement for the young child. This is an achievement which takes place over time: 'Perceptual integration, which is the translation of information from one sense to another, although partly functional at birth, improves with age beyond the childhood years' (Doherty and Bailey 2003, p. 35).

Sensory-motor development: what does this mean?

Motor development can be said to be *movement development*. The word 'motor' also implies a mechanism behind the movement which initiates, causes and then actually carries out that movement. In the human, movement is not a purely mechanistic action. There is a complex process of links, connections and relationships between the sensory systems of the human nervous system and the activation of a muscle to produce movement.

Impulses from the brain travel through the nerve endings to make the muscle react. The blended term 'sensory-motor' implies these links between the sensory systems, the neural networks and the mechanical movement. This term should not be confused with that of *sensori-motor*, coined by Piaget to cover a period of infant intellectual development from birth to eighteen months approximately, a summary of which can be read as an Appendix in Donaldson (1987, p. 134).

As well as the linked actions of the sensory systems, the nervous system and the motor-muscle systems, perceptual aspects also come into play. In an attempt to aid understanding of this complex interplay the simple analogy of the robot can again be helpful.

Inside the robot there are lots of wires and circuits. To make the robot move electrical activity is sent from the computer 'brain' down the wires to activate a movement of, say, the arm. The electrical impulse travels at great speed and is itself invisible. The action of the robot arm is visible. There would be no conscious intention or desire behind the move. The move would be functional and directed: the robot could move to pick up an apple, but it would not be thinking, 'I would like that apple.'

When a human moves an arm, the process is in fact quite similar to that within the robot. There is electrical activity in the brain and impulses travel from the brain along nerve endings to give signals to the muscle. The muscle fibres react and the arm moves: mechanistic movement. In the human this mechanistic movement is often preceded by conscious will, or thought,

perhaps to reach an object. The human may think, 'I would like that apple', and the move could be said to be intentional. Sensory aspects such as sight, touch and distance-judgement will affect the successful move (Figure 2.1).

Some added complexities regarding human movement

Much human movement is either automatic or so well-rehearsed as to seem automatic.

The small baby shows movement stages which are random and lacking in motive, as well as movement which has a motivation and later on a conscious intention. The movement of the baby and the very young child can be said to be *pre-*

Figure 2.1   Intention + motor activity = movement

automatic. As the infant grows, the sensory systems are also developing and maturing.

Although skilled movement in the human can be said to be intentional, the *mechanical act of movement* does not have conscious thought preceding, accompanying or *instructing* the move. The human does not have conscious brain activity which would say, 'Hello, Brain ... send electrical impulses from brain to arm, contract biceps now, reach over, open fingers now, close around apple, etc., etc. ...'. This factor provides much of the difficulty and complexity in the study of motor development and motor skill acquisition, motor organization and motor planning.

Movement requiring this conscious, mental giving of instructions can be seen in stroke patients where the brain has suffered an injury; there is impairment of the central nervous system and the signals, the electrical impulses, which should occur in a flash seem to take an age to transmit. The patient seems to have to will these things to happen and a simple movement can take a very long time to be effected or the movement may not be possible at all. Furthermore, some muscles may be locked in spasm as a result of brain injury: the brain does not work as it should and the signals for muscle tension and release do not transmit. Much can be learned about basic sensory-motor development in young children by observation and study of patients who are older and who have suffered injury, trauma or stroke. The slowing down of the processes in these patients can enable clearer observation for practitioners. Some of the therapeutic exercises

given to the patients use movement as a means to re-educate the neural networks and the 'muscle memory'. The young child will learn through the use of movement in a similar fashion, but it will be experienced in a new, fresh, first-time way.

The perceptual and sensory systems

The sensory systems develop as the young child grows. The development of perceptual awareness enhances *self-awareness* and the establishment of the self-concept. The sensory and perceptual aspects involved are: sight and visual perception; hearing and auditory perception; taste and smell, the olfactory system; touch and tactile perception; balance and the vestibular sense; kinaesthetic perception; proprioceptive perception; spatial perception; and rhythmic awareness.

A basic knowledge of each of these systems, their development in the young child and related terminology is necessary before some understanding can be gained regarding the complex interaction of these systems and the acquisition and refinement of motor skill, movement and co-ordination.

Sight and visual perception

In the first weeks of life, the baby can centre his eyes on an object and track a slowly moving object (Aslin 1981, in Doherty and Bailey 2003, p. 27). The ability to focus more clearly develops during the first year. Very young babies can recognize familiar faces and can mirror expression. As well as presenting the

world to the child, sight is important in relation to spatial awareness and distance judgement. It is also essential as a means to self-awareness, body-awareness and for the skill of copying. Sight, image-processing and labelling are inherent in language development. Visual tracking is the beginning of skill in hand/eye co-ordination. Visual acuity – 'the resolving power of the eye' – (Barber and Legge 1976, p. 22) plus form perception, peripheral vision, 3-D vision and distance perception all develop from the second month of life and continue to improve during the first year. All of these aspects of vision are of vital importance to both motor skill and general intellectual development.

Hearing and auditory perception

From birth the baby can hear sounds and he soon learns to associate them: he hears the voice or steps of his mother approaching and reacts. He is startled by loud, sudden noise. The baby makes sounds too and enjoys being rocked to rhythmic sound-games, songs and rhymes. This rhythmic sound-play experience is vitally important for sensory, intellectual, language and motor development. The baby enjoys sound-toys: rattles and mobiles. The fact that the sound of the toy is initiated by movement is important in terms of motor skill acquisition for the child's learning and also for practitioners studying this field. The baby soon learns that hitting or tapping the mobile produces a sound.

Making meaning from sound is part of auditory perception and is a basis for speech, linguistic,

intellectual and emotional development. Knowing and naming (of people, body parts and objects) contribute to the child's understanding of his world. The toddler begins to learn to sort sounds, to filter out background sound and to listen to what is important. This is increasingly important as the child embarks upon his wider education at nursery and school. Hearing is an inherent part of learning: listening, paying attention and responding appropriately continue to be important through the whole of life. Hearing problems can have marked effects upon behaviour, confidence and the ability to learn. Also, the inner ear mechanism – the vestibular system – affects balance and the efficient functioning of the whole body.

Taste and smell: the olfactory system

Taste and smell affect the feeding of the child and the development of eating habits, and there are obvious relationships between health and nutrition and growth and failure to thrive. From birth the baby exhibits the rooting reflex and suckles and swallows. The actual mechanics of eating and mastication can be affected by physiological weakness and motor development problems (Ripley *et al.* 1998, pp. 56–63). Poor nutrition can have a profound effect upon physical development and health. Social and emotional elements come into play here too, as young children can refuse to eat certain foods or refuse to eat altogether, leading to frustrations developing in child and parent.

The olfactory system helps the child to explore his world. The baby explores objects with his mouth and smells become part of the complicated

information he has to process. He soon learns which things he can eat and which things he likes to eat, and these preferences are often linked with smell. He also learns about what he should not eat: the parental 'No' when he tries to place unsuitable things in his mouth soon becomes understood (between six and nine months).

Olfactory perception and processing are very complex, and it is almost impossible to set out mechanistically what is happening when the human smells a delicious or revolting smell. The brain-response may elicit a body-response, for example, the mouth may water or the stomach might heave before any visual aspects are apprehended. One could wonder whether these responses are learned, conditioned or inherent.

It can be seen that the olfactory system has profound effects upon the health and functioning of the human child and also in his understanding, processing of information and management of the world around him. Confidence in managing eating and related issues such as hygiene and going to the toilet can affect the child's performance at school. The child's toilet training should be fairly well-advanced by the age of four, but factors like anxieties over food management, coping at lunch time, asking and going to the toilets can all be affected and set back by a new environment and people.

Touch and tactile perception

Tactile perception means that the young child can touch and feel things; he is also aware of *being*

touched by other people and by objects. *Simple* tactile perception involves touching and feeling objects and textures and also the perception of touch on his own body.

The more complex aspects of tactile perception relate to the process of making sense of all the different experiences relating to this sense. Touch and feel involve a very complicated interplay between the nerves, the neural network, the brain and an array of motor responses. This interplay results in what could be called *mental learning* and *muscle learning*. If the child touches something which is very hot, there will be an almost instant response: he will withdraw his fingers or drop the object. This rapid withdrawal of the fingers is so fast it resembles a reflex response. If an adult treads upon a drawing pin in bare feet there is an almost instantaneous jumping and lifting of the foot. It seems as thought this sense of touch and response is wired into the humans' systems of safety and self-preservation, and this shows up some of the complexities of this sense. Feelings of pain and of pleasure involve complicated links between sensory awareness and the emotions.

Managing weight and gravity and going against these forces is part of tactile awareness, developing strength awareness and the corresponding successful movement. This fact is not obvious, because as soon as body-awareness and environment-awareness become developed in the very young infant the tactile sensory aspects become so familiar as to become unconscious. For example, the young child soon learns how much

force to apply when lifting, moving and stacking one building brick upon another.

However, for the study of movement competence and motor skill acquisition these factors are of vital importance. Touch and tactile perception combine with elements relating to the vestibular, kinaesthetic and proprioceptive systems (balance, movement and 'feel' respectively) which have effects upon the child's awareness and understanding of his own body, his world around him and on his acquisition and honing of movement skills. This combined relationship governs the extent to which the child becomes a successful operator, learner, mover and manipulator.

Balance and the vestibular sense

Balance is another skill which, once acquired, is taken for granted and which seems to be automatic. Moving requires management of weight, gravity and strength. It involves both going against and going with gravity; walking, for example, requires the controlled shift and suspension of weight and the *loss and regaining of balance*. As adults, we are only consciously aware of our balance system when we lose it because of illness or problems with the inner ear mechanism, or if we try out a brand new sport or skill, such as wind-surfing or ballet dancing.

The beginnings of development of the vestibular sense can be seen in the transitions from the supine baby to the infant managing the weight of his own head and the lifting and turning of the head (in the first months of life). The baby (from two

months) will show attempts to raise his head against gravity. This management should not be underestimated, as the head is very heavy in relation to the rest of the body. The orientation of the head and of the body in space and in height forms part of vestibular sensory awareness and the skill of balance. There is a complex perceptual interplay between the fluid and pressure in the inner ear, the position of the head, the eyes working together and focusing, the moving of the body in space and knowing (sensing) where the body is.

The vestibular sense is not solely concerned with balance. Whole body co-ordination, management of both sides of the body and movements which go across the mid-line of the body are all important aspects. This sense also merges and operates with other sensory systems. Loss of balance, giddiness and the resultant disorientation can make us feel very unwell, as the whole perceptual apparatus seems to be thrown out of kilter. Once again, loss or impairment in function of adults as a result of illness can illuminate study of the development of these functions in the young child.

Balance is also a higher order movement skill, which can be seen in later, more directed movement operations, for example, gymnastic activities (Figure 2.2). Balance and body tension should be understood by practitioners before they go on to teach higher gross motor skills to children. Successful operation at these higher skill levels requires subconscious and, at times, *conscious integration* of the vestibular sensory system,

muscle tension and release, spatial orientation skills and visual perception. It is very interesting that the focus of the eyes affects balance: attempting certain moves and balances with eyes closed can be almost impossible, particularly for the young child: this serves as a good example to illustrate how the sensory systems all work together in synthesis. Practitioners can experience this practical example themselves by walking with eyes closed, along a PE bench or a chalked straight line on the floor. It is difficult to feel confident, to balance and to know when the end of the bench/line is close.

Kinaesthetic perception

Kinaesthetic perception could be defined as an awareness of moving and of movement. Kinaesthesia or kinaesthesis means 'the sense of movement', from the Ancient Greek, *kineein*, to move and *aesthesis*, sensation. The developing

'I can balance …'

'I can feel the bench …'

Figure 2.2   A six-year-old

child begins to know about his own movement and where his limbs are; he feels and knows, 'I have a body'; 'My body moves' (Sherbourne 1993). The child begins to acquire the sense of 'feel', of knowing what his body is doing without looking and of sensing his body's boundary.

Kinaesthetic awareness is also part of learning how much strength and force is needed to carry out certain movements, how to judge distance and to negotiate objects and how to move in the environment. It is the sense of space/body management (orientation in space).

Doing more than one thing at a time in movement terms – for example, running and avoiding furniture – requires relatively sophisticated kinaesthetic sensing. The baby's crawling (nine months to one year of age) is a good example of early kinaesthetic sensing: in crawling the limbs move in opposition, right arm, left leg, left arm, right leg, but the baby does not need to look at his limbs. Other sensory systems work alongside in a complex physiological/neurological interplay which contributes to formation of movement memory. Some children with special needs and movement problems cannot crawl without looking, even when they are older, reaching eleven years plus. It seems, therefore, that oppositional movement implies complex sensory/neural/kinaesthetic functioning – as do movements which cross the mid-line of the body (right arm crossing and moving over the left side of body). To attempt to explain this simply, it seems that part of the reason behind this is that the right hemisphere of the brain controls the left side of the body and the left hemisphere controls movement

on the right, and these crossover skills do take time to assimilate. The 'Brain Gym' exercises devised by Dennison and Dennison (1994) work upon these principles.

Knowing how to move efficiently and smoothly, without extraneous movements or effort and without bumping into other people or objects in the environment, is part of kinaesthetic awareness. Some adults have a poorly developed version of this sense and cannot judge if they are invading the personal space of others. Conversely, some adults cannot cope with close contact or with being touched by others. Taking part in dance and movement exercises can help adults to develop their kinaesthetic sensing, in the same ways as these activities are invaluable for young children.

Proprioceptive perception

The word 'proprioceptive' – from the Latin for 'own' and 'to receive' – can be said to mean feeling and understanding one's own sensory signals and stimuli. The muscles and joints are equipped with these proprioceptors. Stimuli received by these receptors results in a sensory reaction. According to the *Chambers English Dictionary* (1990), a receptor is 'an element of the nervous system adapted for reception of stimuli ...'

The proprioceptive system is a feedback system which gives sense and awareness of muscular position: in simple terms, feeling and knowing the positioning of one's body and body parts – knowing without having to look (Ripley *et al*, 1998). Proprio-

ceptive perception is very closely allied to kinaesthetic perceptions and is part of it. The adult working at his computer knows that his bottom is on his chair and his back is touching the back-rest, yet he does not need to pay particular attention to these factors; he does not need to look and check. The sensing of the two systems (proprioceptive and kinaesthetic) is utilized when a person runs up and down stairs without having to look at them. The person is sensing the position of each step in relation to body movement.

> *Children who have a sound proprioceptive sense can sit down without looking at the chair – they sense where it is, how high the seat is and therefore accurately gauge the amount of effort needed to sit down ... even fastening buttons can be done by feel alone.*
> Macintyre (2000, p. 43)

All conscious movement, particularly movement with an intention, utilizes the proprioceptive system. Effective movement uses 'feedforward' (Rosenbaum 1991, p. 15) from the receptors as well as feedback. For example, a tall adult learns to judge if he is about to hit his head on a low doorway lintel. If he senses that he may hit his head he will duck (feedforward). He may know from past, painful experience (feedback) that he has hit his head on doorways like this one.

To make links with tactile awareness and to exercise these sensory skills, the child can play at blindfolded guessing games of familiar objects or with a feely bag; he can recognize what he is touching and feeling. Past experience (feedback) enables him to know and guess (feedforward).

Physical Development in the Early Years

Spatial perception

The young child needs to develop an awareness of his own body space and the space around him in the immediate environment. Spatial perception is more complex than the term suggests: spacing, moving, effort, relationships, safety, lateral and directional awareness are all important aspects. Spatial perception increases in scope and size as the infant develops and his world view enlarges. The baby only *knows* what is in his immediate body-environment, whereas the world of the two-year-old is really beginning to open up. Spatial awareness and management of the body and objects in space are skills which continue to develop throughout life; these skills are practised every time a new sport or game is encountered.

First of all, the infant develops an awareness of his own body-space. A true awareness of personal space develops over time, into adulthood; indeed, some adults have a very poor sense of personal space. This immediate body-space is called the *kinaesphere* (American or German spelling, *kinesphere*), a term devised by Rudolf Laban in 1948 in his system of movement analysis: 'Around the body is the "sphere of movement", or "Kine-sphere"' (Laban 1988, p. 85). It can be helpful to call this 'bubble space' when working with children.

Second, the infant experiences his movement within the immediate environment, in 'room space'. As soon as he can, at around nine months of age, the infant begins to explore his immediate space and different ways of travelling in it; he begins by

travelling on the floor 'by rolling, wriggling on abdomen or crawling' and by the age of four years he 'Navigates self-locomotion skilfully, turning sharp corners, running, pushing and pulling' (Sheridan 1995, pp. 13 and 35). This progression shows increasing awareness of direction, forwards, backwards and sideways movement, and of pathways around the space and objects or people in it. In his investigations of spatial awareness, the child needs to know which way up he is and which way he is facing. Therefore, the young child should explore and experiment with appropriate ways of being upside down and of feeling his weight upon the floor.

Judgement of distance requires the use of visual and proprioceptive sensing. Many parents observe first hand the toddler experiencing space management as he bumps his head underneath the table. He soon learns to judge (without looking) the space around the table and under it. The child learns how to place a cup on a table: this requires judgements of strength, weight and force as well as balance and spatial awareness – quite an achievement. When the cup has liquid in it this presents even more of a challenge. Again, it can be seen that efficient movement and functioning require blends of senses and motor skills working in synthesis. This can be seen when the toddler is feeding himself and when he uses a real cup instead of a feeding cup; he is learning to judge where his mouth is and how to manage implements and objects in space and in relation to his body.

More skilled spatial perception means that the child develops an awareness of laterality, knowing

which is his right and left side and what his right or left hand may be doing; he also begins to develops a preference for using one hand. Another more complicated spatial management skill is an awareness of directionality, which means that the child has an understanding of his own personal direction orientation, together with an understanding of which way objects and other people are facing, plus an understanding of right and left in others. Activities with mirrors and mirroring a partner's movements offer valuable opportunities for exploration of these aspects. Confident management of orientation takes time to develop and may still not be soundly established in an eleven-year-old (or in some instances in adults).

Rhythmic awareness

Although not a sensory system in its own right, this is an important aspect of sensory-motor development and involves many sensory elements: auditory, tactile, kinaesthetic and proprioceptive.

Rhythmic awareness is a natural part of being alive; humans feel the rise and fall breath rhythms and heart beat pulse of their own bodies. Rhythmic sensing is part of natural timing and can contribute towards an awareness of pattern and repetition, which are both important movement concepts. During her research into movement development in infants, Thelen (1995, p. 83) noted the cyclical, repetitive nature of many actions, causing her to comment that 'rhythmicity is a fundamental property of the human motor system'.

Experiencing and moving to rhythms aids the acquisition of inner, 'felt' timing, which is an aspect of efficiency in both basic movements and more complex movement patterns. It can be very interesting to watch infants responding to strong, rhythmic music. Also, young children can find it almost impossible to be still when experiencing lively music.

This inner-timing sense affects whole body management and is an essential higher dance skill. Although some basic rhythmic sensing can be said to be innate, and many people seem to have a very good in-built sense of timing and rhythm, other people have difficulties with these aspects throughout life. Language has its own rhythms, patterns, troughs and peaks just like movement, and young children enjoy experimenting with sounds, words, patterns, rhymes and rhythms. Enacting, remembering and acquiring confidence in action songs and rhymes contribute towards this complex form of sensory-motor learning.

Sensory learning and motor learning: a synthesis

The perceptual systems work with and upon the mechanical functioning of the body to produce movement responses and actions. The synthesis is very complex, and all systems affect and impinge upon each other. Intellectual, social and emotional functioning are also developing alongside. By referring to the perceptual systems outlined above, it can be seen which sensory systems are involved in particular types of movement. Certain skills seem

to be automatically acquired, while others need to be met and exercised at appropriate stages of physical development.

The different sensory systems are involved in the development of motor functioning, facility and all movement skill. Movement learning can also enhance sensory development. The human child shows how sophisticated processing and motor skills develop from early perceptual 'sensing' as he makes progress in and sense of his world. Moving and operating successfully and developing personal confidence, sensitivity and sensibility is an astounding achievement.

Young children are excited by their growing mastery of their own bodies, all of their senses and of their environment (Figure 2.3), and enjoy exercising their skills and meeting new challenges.

We can ...

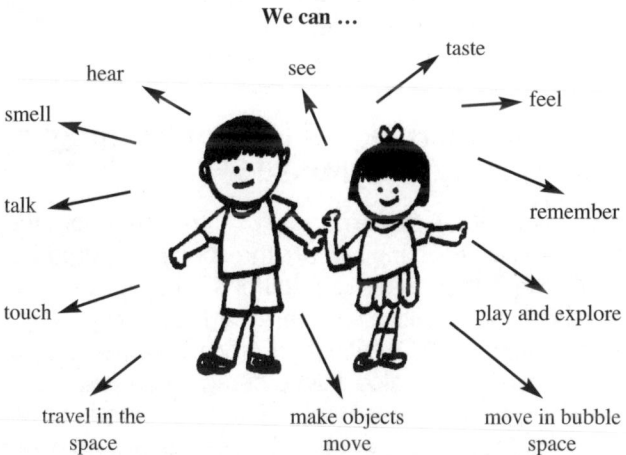

Figure 2.3   Ready to meet new challenges

3

Motor Skill Development

What are motor skills and why are they important?

All voluntary movement requires the use of motor skills. The motor skill can be thought of as the initiation of and the mechanical potential behind the movement. It is important to be very clear here about the differences between the terms 'motor' and 'movement', as they are often used interchangeably or in a vague manner.

It can be useful to think of 'motor' as meaning having the potential for movement to result. However, keeping still, stability and lack of movement also form part of motor skill. Muscle tone and strength are required to maintain posture and stability, in other words, to hold the body still. It is therefore important that terms are used with care and precision. The introduction and explanation of a new term (motor string) and the clarification of existing terminology should prove helpful.

Motor strings: an explanation

Motor responses in the muscles come from nerve impulses: the muscle reacts and initiates a single

movement, for example, the bicep muscle shortens and contracts and the forearm is lifted. In a more complex movement, a whole string of responses is involved. For example, when several impulses travel to several muscles (a motor string) almost like an electrical chain reaction – shoulder, upper arm, forearm, wrist and hand – a reaching movement is carried out. Several joined mini-moves take place in this reaching: reaching is an example of a movement pattern.

Several linked motor responses (a *motor string*) can be said to be the means by which a complex movement (a *movement pattern*) is achieved.

Movement patterns

More complicated movements, when several small moves are joined, are movement patterns. Reaching for an apple is an example of a movement pattern. Reaching and grabbing the apple, kicking a football or bowling a cricket ball show other, more complex examples of movement patterns.

The robot analogy is again helpful in providing a simplified view. If the robot were to be required to draw back one of its legs and then to strike a ball with its foot in order to direct the ball forwards, then it would have to be given several separate, sequenced movement commands from a control panel or computer. It may take some time to input the list of commands. This programmed string of commands could be said to be the potential for

movement (the motor string) and the commands would have to be sequenced in a linear, consecutive manner. The resultant movement would be the robot 'kick' (a movement pattern). In a human child, the same sort of programme of commands would be given, but the transmission to the result (from the brain-computer via the nerves to the correct muscles) would be almost instantaneous. Also, in practised moves, the linear sequencing (motor organization) would not be conscious or evident.

Gross and fine motor skills expanded

Motor skills are the potential for planned, organized movement and for body stability, and can be classed simply as gross motor skills and fine motor skills. Gross motor skills involve large, whole body movements, locomotion (travelling) and whole body stretches. Fine motor skills involve smaller movements, manipulative skills and isolation of body parts. Running would be an example of a gross motor skill, using scissors of a fine motor skill.

All of the perceptual systems set out in Chapter 2 affect gross and fine motor skills: the acquisition of them, their execution and refinement. All motor skill execution can be improved with repetition and practice and, as motor skill improves, perceptual acuity is enhanced; in other words, practice of motor skill develops and exercises a range of senses. This two-way interchange of learning is an important point for practitioners to consider.

Cameo

Sean is five years old. He is not enjoying his time at school. He has very poor listening skills and he seems unable to sit still for many seconds. He often calls out in the classroom. He seems to rush from one activity to the next and does not complete tasks. He appears to spoil activities and carpet time on purpose and the other children do not like him very much. He likes to organize the plates and food in the class café and he enjoys outdoor activities. He is not experiencing much satisfaction in the classroom as he seems unable to settle to any activity for longer than a few seconds. He is very agile in terms of gross motor skills, but he does do things at top speed.

What could be done to help Sean to slow down a little and to experience success? How could the practitioner build upon Sean's abilities, yet at the same time introduce activities which could influence slowing down and fostering a little more care regarding his surroundings and other children? Could activities be devised which might help the development of sensory awareness and so aid task management and success and satisfaction?

As Sean's gross motor skills are fairly sound, he could be given activities which involve watching and copying ('Simon Says' without words). If careful copying formed part of gaining a point in the game,

Sean would have to slow down, watch and concentrate. He could be asked to demonstrate successful dribbling with a football around three cones. He could be given an important job in the café (preparing a meal and drink for an adult to try). He might be given a picture card to mark his own special place to sit on the carpet. He could be asked to show another child how he prepared the plastic 'meal' in the café and to tell everyone about it at carpet time. Asking Sean to show others his achievements will mean that he encounters satisfaction, pride and confidence at school and that he has to utilize sensory awareness, selecting from his bank of motor skills in order to be successful.

How are skills acquired and learned?

It is very helpful to think of the learning of physical skills as a three-part process. The three parts of the process are as follows:

1. *Acquisition* The skill (for example, walking) has in the first instance to be acquired. Following the very first try, subsequent attempts gradually improve.

2. *Development* With time and repeated application, the skill develops, becomes improved, and its execution is smoother.

3. *Consolidation/habituation* As the skill is practised and revisited many times, it becomes honed and consolidated. Eventually, the skill becomes second nature, internalized, habitual: it becomes ingrained in muscle memory. Effort and conscious application diminish as the

process moves towards consolidation, and the skill appears to be automatic.

This three-part process is very important for practitioners to consider, along with a product of applying the skill (a successful step or series of steps, in the example of walking). Both process and product are important in physical learning and in a physical education. It is vital for practitioners to understand this learning process as it underpins the ways in which skills are to be introduced and taught to children and ties in with how children learn in the physical domain. Therefore, practitioners should break down skills into sub-skills and teach one simple part before another is linked: for example, the six-year-old child should stand still, dropping and catching a ball with both hands, before attempting to bounce the ball and travel (working towards pat-bouncing and dribbling). Also, children should revisit skills many times.

Enhanced performance: co-ordination and body tension

As the child learns new skills and works through the process outlined above, he gains mastery of basic skills of body management such as walking and running (basic locomotion). He goes on to attempt more complex skills and skill-blends, for example, skipping, running and kicking a football. It is important that his attempts match his developmental stage and his capabilities.

The young child finds doing several things at once difficult. He will use his whole body to do things (as in

catching a large ball by bending down and embracing it) and find isolations (using only his fingers and arms) difficult. Practise over time will enable the child to minimize extraneous, unnecessary movements. Putting together appropriate moves and managing speed and response are part of more effective performance. These are improvements which Sean, from the cameo above, should show in his subsequent endeavours.

Co-ordination is part of improved function: it can be described as an ability to link moves and movement patterns together smoothly, utilizing balance, stability and timing, with no extraneous movements. It means that several things are happening at once. Co-ordination means that both fine and gross motor skills can work together (this can be seen, for example, in playing netball).

Body tension is an important aspect relating to more skilled movement performance and balance, and is a natural aptitude in *some* people. Body tension means that the inner core of the body, the centre, is strong and that the body is 'lifted' in correct posture or true alignment. It requires strength in the back and abdomen; a slumping, slouching body is showing no body tension at all. Correct posture and good body tension can be encouraged in children as they become more confident in movement, at around six or seven years of age. Very young children should not be pushed into working with artificial body tension, although some will possess it naturally.

Enhanced gross motor performance requires development of strength, control, whole body

management and agility. Enhanced fine motor performance requires dexterity, tactile and visual awareness and proprioceptive functioning. (Interestingly, the root meaning of the word dexterity is 'right', from the Latin, implying that right-handedness is synonymous with adroitness and skill.)

Categories of motor skills

Motor skills and the resultant movements can be categorized and grouped under headings in order to aid understanding. It is suggested that practitioners use these categories when they are planning experiences, work and tasks for children. The five headings are: defeating gravity and obtaining stability; non-locomotor skills; locomotor skills; spatial awareness; and manipulative and fine management skills. Expansion of these categories shows that various types of movements require a mix of motor skills.

Defeating gravity and obtaining stability

In order to stand, the infant has to develop adequate muscle strength to defeat gravity, attain stability and maintain equilibrium. He also uses gravity in order to move, when he shuffles, crawls and walks: he works against gravity to lift a limb or his head and body weight and with gravity to replace that weight or limb, using an appropriate amount of force.

He also learns to use this gravity/force management when he holds an object: when he is first given a toy to grasp his arm will fall down with the weight of the object, but from six months onwards

he learns how much force to apply so that he can *hold* it. Dexterity also develops as he learns how to manipulate toys using both hands. Gravity has to be defeated when he places one object on top of another, for instance, a block on a small table or when he lifts food to his mouth. Visual and spatial skills are also required to do these things.

Sitting well and standing well, maintaining stability and balance and 'good' walking (matching with reaching the expected developmental milestone within a reasonable time allowance) are important indicators of developing motor skills. Problems with these aspects can indicate the possibility of neuro-physical problems. Mature walking, which involves placing down the heel and then rolling through the ball of the foot onto the toes, requires the co-ordination of complex movement patterns and management of skeletal equilibrium, and is indeed a remarkable physical achievement for the young child.

Stability, maintaining equilibrium, balance and mid-torso strength all contribute to body tension, and these factors affect movement facility when the child takes part in PE lessons at school. Riding a scooter, balancing on a beam and performing a forward roll are all instances of managing gravity and utilizing balance skills.

Non-locomotor skills

Non-locomotor skills are seen in movements which take place in one's own body space, in 'bubble space'. This is the first space that the tiny baby explores. The older child experiments with

reaching, stretching and bending movements which can be done sitting or standing and which are examples of execution of non-locomotor skills. The movements can be called *rooted* or *on the spot*.

Locomotor skills

Locomotor skills are travelling skills. They take the individual around, off the spot, literally meaning 'moving' (*motor*) to and from 'places' (*loco*) in the Latin. The movements (such as walking, running and skipping) involve use of gross motor skills and space and force judgements. Gravity, weight and balance management skills come into play at the same time, as does visual processing as the individual looks for obstacles and other people in the space.

Spatial awareness

Spatial awareness merits separate consideration as it is so important and interlinks with several other aspects. Spatial awareness covers an understanding of self and body boundary, as well as awareness and management of both personal ('bubble') and environmental ('room') space. Proprioceptive sensing and visual perception together with speed/distance judgements are all required to negotiate the obstacles and other people encountered.

Awareness of one's own body is a first example of spatial skill development: the baby realizes he has toes and feet and a body and he can sense where they are. He realizes: 'I have a body'; 'I am me'. He begins to form a self-concept.

Spatial awareness, management and under-standing are necessary when relationships are being explored: the baby realizing his mother has left the room, the toddler passing a toy to a friend and the seven-year-old mirroring his partner in gymnastic activities are all examples of this. These examples show that as well as the physical elements, emotional, social and intellectual aspects are important.

As the child explores the space around him, non-locomotor aspects of space are discovered – for instance, exploring and understanding levels has links with language: high, low, up, down, near, far. Locomotor aspects are important when travelling in space, managing distance, speed, objects and turns. Spatial understanding affects use of force or effort, for instance, when rolling a ball at a close object or partner, or at a target or partner further away.

Manipulative and fine management skills

Manipulative and fine management skills are fine motor skills. The skills are to do with development of fine control, small movements and the management of objects. The term 'manipulative' actually means the use of the hands; however, management in this context can be taken to mean investigating, moving and controlling an object: this could be done with a foot or the toes or with parts of the mouth. Play activity with crayons (precursor to drawing and writing) and experience of handling cutlery and exploring and eating different foods are examples of this aspect of motor skill development.

Physical Development in the Early Years

Fine control, dexterity, coping with visual and proprioceptive clues, managing pressure, and force judgements all form part of this area of skill. Tactile awareness also comes into play. A baby will mouth objects to feel them and this means that he has mastered the skill of putting things into his mouth, using body-, space- and distance-awareness: he 'knows' where his mouth is. A four-year-old rolling a ball to a partner needs to judge direction, sense the timing to release the object from his fingers and know how much force to apply when he sends it.

Manipulative skills cover holding, grasping and gripping objects and tools. The pincer grip, which involves intricate finger-thumb management, is still developing in children above three years of age. Delicate operations, such as coping with fasteners, buttons and zips in dressing and undressing, require concentration and dexterity.

The word 'manipulation' also has another meaning which is important here, the intention to make something do what is required or desired. Play activities with a wide range of toys allow the child to work on manipulating objects by making them behave in certain ways; for instance, putting pegs through holes, building, doing a simple jigsaw. Later activities in skills which are games-based also use this skill, such as throwing a ball, using a bat and ball, directing the ball where required. This skill is usually required in specific games in order to score a goal or to hit a target. All of these activities show that manual, tactile and visual linking is taking place. This linking forms the beginning of hand/eye co-ordination.

Examination of the five categories/groupings of motor skills listed above shows that none of the aspects works in isolation. All aspects of motor and movement skill involve perceptual information and processing. Practitioners wishing to focus upon certain skills for particular children can plan experiences which cover one or two of the groupings. Other aspects can be pruned away. For instance, a child with poor visual tracking and manipulative skills can *sit down* opposite a partner to play at rolling and trapping a ball. This would mean that the travelling, balancing, and space negotiation aspects were removed, allowing greater concentration on the skills which are most in need of development.

A chronological review of motor skills

It may be helpful to sum up by looking at the relevant physical and perceptual skills from a chronological perspective, using the five categories of skills explored above. Forming realistic expectations of children at particular ages enables practitioners to plan activities which support particular skills through the three-part process of skill acquisition, development and consolidation. Table 3.1 shows an outline of the skills developing from birth to two years.

Movement and physical 'exercise' begin as a natural part of life: the baby moves, cries, kicks and exercises himself at will. From the first months into the second and third years' the child carries out

Physical Development in the Early Years

Skills category	Examples	Skill type
1. Defeating gravity	Lifting head, sitting, crawling, standing	Gross motor
2. Non-locomotor	Waving/kicking arms, legs, twisting, turning, reaching	Gross motor
3. Locomotor	Crawling, walking	Gross motor
4. Spatial awareness	Knowing immediate space	Gross, fine sensory motor blends
5. Manipulative	Grasping, holding, tapping	Fine motor

Table 3.1   Skills: birth to two years

exploration of his close environment, using all his senses. What he can do in it and how he can move and travel form his play exercise.

Table 3.2 shows an outline of the skills picture from three to five years.

During the 'toddler' stages, the child's environment (both the indoor and the outdoor) expands. He will encounter (with adult support) water and sand play, the paddling pool, the park, the swimming pool. He experiments and learns at an incredible rate. He is very inquisitive and lively and needs constant supervision in a safe, secure space. He learns through movement, and this can be seen quite clearly. He enjoys adding to his travelling skills. As he plays with a range of objects, toys, media, music and sounds he is extending his sensory experiences and developing rhythmic awareness.

From three to five years, the child's physical

Skills category	Examples	Skill type
1. Defeating gravity	Jumping, hopping, twisting, swim play, tricycle, bike and scooter riding	Gross motor
2. Non-locomotor	Stretching, turning, moving body parts, being low, high, big, small	Gross motor
3. Locomotor	Range of travelling, on and around apparatus	Gross motor
4. Spatial awareness	Directional awareness, distance judgement	Gross, fine sensory motor blends
5. Manipulative	Building, threading, mark making, colouring, sending, capturing ball	Fine motor

Table 3.2   Skills: three to five years

skills development and physical competence really extend. Several basic locomotor skills are consolidated and internalized by this stage. Non-locomotor skills diversify and locomotor skill repertoire increases. The child will enjoy exercising his skills of anti-gravity and weight management in different forms of jumping, climbing, tumbling, rolling and riding. He will experience a range of environments, new people and differing social settings. His language skills and vocabulary are extended in the circumstances of increased social interaction.

Between six and eight years, the skills repertoires become much broader and the wide differences in

skill competence between individual children become very marked. Skills competence in terms of travelling, balance, co-ordination, implement and object management becomes more consolidated. 'Sensory' learning becomes less obvious, because sensory awareness has become internalized to a great extent. Fine and gross motor skill prowess is improving during these years as basic writing, drawing, movement and games skills are extended, exercised and honed. An outline of the skills development from six to eight years is presented in Table 3.3.

Skills category	Examples	Skill type
1. Defeating gravity	Jumping, leaping, swim activities, tricycle, bike and scooter riding	Gross motor
2. Non-locomotor	Understanding levels, direction, strong shapes, stretches, twisting, curling	Gross motor
3. Locomotor	Enjoying a range of travelling, speeds, apparatus, equipment, joining, sequencing	Gross motor
4. Spatial awareness	Understanding directional awareness, distance judgement	Gross, fine sensory motor blends
5. Manipulative	Art, craft, design activities, writing, drawing, practical maths, science	Fine motor

Table 3.3   Skills: six to eight years

Movement organization and movement planning

Whenever a child carries out a movement pattern such as reaching for an apple, or rolling a ball, it is vital that the mini-moves which make up the pattern are done in the right order. This is called *seriation*. This ordering can be mentally rehearsed: as an adult would do when learning to strike a golf ball for the first time.

It can be said that a simple movement pattern (when a baby, for instance, waves his arm and hits a musical mobile) has a form of movement organization behind the action. The action, repetition and trial-and-error experiences mean that the baby learns to carry out the moves in the correct order to strike the mobile. The baby is not, however, mentally ordering, rehearsing or planning his movement. Movement organization is acquired through experience and it is *part of the experience*.

The very young child does not carry out this mental ordering and organization. He learns by experience, by repeated effort, by trial and error, and feels when the right result occurs. He learns to carry out a form of movement organization based upon his sensory experiences and the success (or failure) of his movements. As the child's experience extends and he learns by repeated successes and failures, he acquires the feel of a successful endeavour and this can form the basis for movement organization. The child may talk to himself as he carries out the moves, although this 'self-talk' (Vygotsky in Keenan 2002, p. 37) gradually becomes internalized.

Physical Development in the Early Years

The child may be given parental instruction and demonstration to aid him. As he gets older and his movement activities become more challenging, he starts to use more directed help and, together with his own experiential learning, he can begin to use a form of movement planning. He would probably start to do this mental planning and ordering in a simple form from around four or five years of age. As he can listen to direction, so can he mentally give himself direction. This movement planning is necessary when several movement patterns and actions are linked into a sequence, as, for example, when the child is going to hop along a bench, jump off the end and land softly on a mat.

The focus of this chapter has been on physical skills, how they are developed and how they become consolidated and internalized. Practitioners can build upon their knowledge of the types of skills and the process of acquisition, development and consolidation of these skills in order to plan and select appropriate activities for children. Practitioners can also use their understanding of the processes of simple movement organization leading to movement planning to assist children with seriation of movements. If practitioners use strategies to slow down the action, for example, rolling a ball rather than throwing it, it can give the child time to assimilate the ordering, the movements themselves and the outcomes.

4

How Children Learn in the Physical Domain

Active learning

As has been seen, a baby experiences his world and learns in a physical, sensory way. It could be said that he learns through movement and through his senses. He continues to learn in this way, through experience and action (experiential learning), throughout life.

Being able to learn and being ready to learn depend upon developmental and social factors. Consequently, practitioners need to be able to plan and build not only upon theoretical background knowledge, but also upon observations of real children. Experiences for each child need to be matched to physique and physical maturity as well as to the expected developmental and movement skill levels: asking a five-year-old to play mini-tennis with a bat and ball when the child has insufficient trapping, directing or manipulative skills is equivalent to giving him *War and Peace* to read!

Nature and nurture

Cameo

A group of four-year-olds are playing in the outdoor classroom, using a range of equipment. Some of the children are tall, strong, agile and seem confident in movement 'for their age', whilst others are of slight build, seem to tire very easily and are anxious about trying new things. Four of the children are overweight for their height, lack energy and application and seem listless. Three children are lithe, rather hyperactive, yet skilful and they hurtle around, never staying long on any of the pieces of apparatus or equipment. Some children are playing alone, others are in pairs and the three 'speed merchants' are playing in a loose group formation, coming together periodically to shout and show off their achievements.

All of the children in the cameo are around four years of age, yet physically they are very different. They have all passed the expected 'milestones', yet they present such a range of differences to an observing practitioner. These differences are in physique, application and attitudes. Factors of maturation, growth, nutrition and health are important and are affected by the home background of each child. The general physique and personality of the child is a result of genetic makeup, i.e. *nature*,

but environmental, social and emotional aspects and experience also affect the child (*nurture*).

Every child brings something particular and unique to the setting; the sensitive practitioner knows that each child has special, particular needs. In every group there will be a range similar to that observed in the four-year-olds discussed above. The ways to begin to help the children and to enhance their abilities and skills can seem very daunting to the beginning practitioner. Aspects relating to nature and nurture are important and influential. In addition, developmental factors can be influenced by good practice, and appropriate interventions can enhance skill acquisition, overall development and confidence in every child.

It does seem that in some circumstances the human child can learn by himself: some physical skills and movement 'milestones' are achieved as a matter of natural course. The infant seems to learn by himself how to hold up his head and how to grab furniture to help him to stand. No one actually tells him how to walk. Trial and error and learning by accident seem to be natural ways of learning.

However, many elements of learning need adult intervention and help. Maturational aspects alone are not sufficient:

> *Maturation provides a young child with the ability to perform a specific movement skill at a very low level of performance. It is only with continuous practice and instruction that a child's level of performance will increase.*
>
> Seefeldt (1984, in Poest *et al.* 1990, p. 5)

It can be seen that aspects of nature alone (the child simply growing and maturing physically) are not enough: the human infant is indeed a tiny learning machine, but real learning involves both action and interaction (with other people, the environment and with objects). As David (1999, p. 7) points out: 'Young children seem to have dispositions to learn different things, they are not simply bundles of biological urges slowly being transformed, as they pass through universal pre-set stages of development, until they become fully formed humans as adults.' The key for the practitioner is to exploit these dispositions at appropriate times and in relevant ways.

The situation regarding experiential learning is complex and adult assistance is necessary. However, knowing when to intervene, how to offer guidance and how to move the child forward to the next learning step can be difficult for inexperienced practitioners. The types of experience and the ways in which children learn can be classified into different modes of learning. Understanding these modes can help practitioners to select appropriate skill challenges and tasks. Further consideration of how an infant learns can be very illuminating in this respect.

How does the small child learn?

No one actually tells the baby how to reach and hold a teething ring or toy, but these objects are provided for him and put before him, but just out of

reach. This is a really important, yet simple, point when considering how children learn. It can be seen to fit with several aspects of learning theory propounded by educationalists and psychologists from the twentieth century such as Piaget (1971), Bruner (1983), Vygotsky (1978), Donaldson (1978), Wood (1976) and others (all discussed in David, 1999).

Some relevant learning theories: a basic summary

Modern educational methods are founded upon an understanding of the young child as an *active* experiential learner – a learner who learns from, processes and makes meaning from practical, first-hand engagement with his surroundings. This engagement takes the form of play: play is the child's 'work' and 'exercise'. A Piagetian view would be that experience is extended as the child passes through stages of development; thus, through active involvement and interaction learning takes place and experience expands.

Building upon experience and extending learning, together with growth of language, make up major elements in the work of Bruner and Vygotsky, where the responsibility for providing the necessary environment for learning falls on the adult close to the child (the adult as *guide*, *facilitator*) providing a *scaffolding* for learning. The next learning 'step' takes place because the 'bridge' is provided by the adult: this illustrates Vygotsky's concept of the *zone of proximal development*, which can be defined as the gap between what the

child can do alone and what he can do with adult support. If the gap is too wide and there is no bridge provided, the child cannot learn; he cannot make the leap.

It is helpful to tease out the different modes of learning in order to investigate how young children learn. Most of the learning of the infant and young child takes place in the physical domain. This learning is *physical* and is based on movement, resulting in a special kind of knowing, *knowing how to do things*, which Bruner (1966) called 'enactive representation' or 'knowledge based in action' (in Harris and Butterworth 2002, p. 29). Experiential learning involves many interlinked sensory systems, in which other forms of learning take place: for example, visual, tactile and aural processing are all forms of learning. The brain, intellectual functioning and cognitive development are involved with this physical learning: memory skills, listening, paying attention, sifting out what is important, speech development and sensory processing are complex forms of brain activity.

Modes of learning

The modes of learning are set out in Table 4.1 and are explained below, accompanied by some practical examples.

1. *Accidental learning* is the first type of learning that the baby experiences and it is a very important form of learning.

ACCIDENTAL LEARNING

CAUSAL LEARNING

EXPERIMENTAL LEARNING

IMITATIVE LEARNING

DEMONSTRATION-BASED LEARNING

INSTRUCTION FOLLOWING

PHYSICAL MANIPULATION

Table 4.1   Modes of learning

Cameo

Baby Steffi is in her cot. She has a duck mobile stretched across the top rail of her cot. Steffi waves her arms and a flail of her arm catches one of the ducks. She continues to wave her arms and catches the mobile several times. Steffi soon learns that her actions make the mobile respond and she really enjoys this activity. She learns how to do this, enjoys it and repeats the action on purpose.

This accidental learning (in the first instance) becomes purposeful learning with a movement-based cause and effect. 'Repetition' and 'enjoyment' are two key words for practitioners to take from this form of learning and to utilize in the planning of learning activities.

2. *Causal learning* (cause and effect) is an extension of accidental learning and utilizes motivation. Success (in result and in executing a skill) and motivation are linked. When the infant crawls (at around nine months), his horizons and the potential for learning expand. He sees objects and shows a conscious desire to reach them; conscious will is exercised. He has already encountered accidental cause and effect learning (where an action of his has an interesting and enjoyable result). He now goes on to expand this by having an actual desire behind the cause.

   The infant striking a soft ball which makes a ringing sound can be a good example: he may strike the ball by accident at first and notices the ball's movement and sound, and then repeat the strike action as he realizes he has caused the sound and movement. He learns that his strike had an enjoyable result and repeats his action: he has learned a simple striking, causal action. In causal learning *trial-and-error* methods are important. The three-year-old trying out kicking skills with a football is taking part in a form of causal learning.

3. *Experimental learning* is another mode of learning which involves trial and error. This way of learning takes place as the infant explores his environment as he plays. Exploratory, experimental play activity has a vital place in the physical education of the young child. Parents and practitioners need to appreciate the value of this free, exploratory play and ensure that there

is plenty of time and space for it to take place and that colourful, exciting toys and items are accessible.

Another type of play, guided play, is where the parent and/or practitioner is more closely involved and guides the activity with a learning objective in mind. During the toddler stages the child's learning potential widens: it is through these stages that adult intervention and guidance are really vital. This means that the growing infant encounters his first experience of being 'taught': as the adult encourages, guides and praises him the child may modify his behaviour and movements.

The child learns from free exploration and from guided play: he tries things, he experiments and he learns from his experimenting.

4. *Imitative learning* uses copying. This is a very important and productive mode for young children and one which practitioners should exploit in their planning. As soon as he can perceive his environment, the young child encounters aspects of everyday life which he copies in his play: for example, washing up or hammering. He learns by copying, from imitation. Copying successful skill execution can be done from general observation or from more targeted observation of a particular demonstration (for instance, learning how to gasp in mock surprise is acquired from general copying; kicking a football may be copied from Dad's demonstration).

This mode of learning is one which continues to be important throughout life. It depends upon

observation and is a successful mode of learning if visual acuity and processing are sound. (Obviously, execution does not always match the modelling: it can be frustrating for the child to try and copy an 'expert' when the wrong moves seem to come out.)

5. *Demonstration-based learning* also depends upon observation. The adult may use an actual demonstration to show the child, which may be accompanied by instructional speech (just as the young child often talks to himself as he is playing, as he is exploring: self-talk).

   Other children may also be the source of the demonstration. Practitioners may set up a 'formal' type of demonstration. 'Everyone watch John's lovely stretched-out roll.' Alternatively, one child may see another child do something and copy the action, or one child may 'teach' another. This mode of learning is an extension of simple copying.

6. *Instruction following* is a different form from simple demonstration. Instruction following can exist alone or the child may learn from instruction following which accompanies a demonstration. This mode also utilizes copying, as well as listening skills, and is useful when the child is older. The child has to focus and pay attention. This mode is an extension of mode 5 (demonstration-based learning).

   An example could be when the teacher asks a class of eight-year-olds to jog on the spot. An example of instructions accompanied by

demonstration would be the teacher talking and showing a seven-year-old how to hold a hockey stick and how to tap the ball.

7. *Physical manipulation techniques* may be employed by the parent or the practitioner to help the child. For example, the parent may grasp the baby's hands and *show* him how to clap by moving his hands to play 'Pat-a-cake', or the parent or practitioner may guide the child to bend his head and body into the correct curve and guide his forward roll. This mode of learning can be employed for more complex operations: for example, tying shoelaces.

Consideration of these modes of learning is important. All depend upon learning by experience, which continues to be important throughout the child's education and into adult life. The modes of learning are set out in this chapter in a sequence which at times refers to chronological development, to show how one mode grows out from another, but they should not be viewed as having hierarchical or chronological sequencing, because different skills utilize different modes.

For example, accidental learning is a productive form of learning for older children and for adults. Also, an adult learning a new skill or sport would utilize all or some of the modes of learning. Some modes are more suitable for certain types of activity and are applicable only when the child has reached appropriate levels of mental and physical maturity. For instance, it would be inappropriate to expect a two-year-old child to learn to use scissors through

the mode of verbal instruction. Both the skill level (fine motor) and the mode are inappropriate. Similarly, written instructions are not suitable unless the child is fairly proficient in reading; indeed, many adults find that learning from written instructions is very difficult. It would seem that physical skills are best encountered and learned in a physical, experiential manner.

The modes presented here are particular to physical and sensory-motor learning, and were devised as a result of a research project over one school year with Year One children (Woodfield 1992). It is helpful if practitioners themselves experience the modes of learning from personal practical involvement in a physical education course. Then the complexities and links can be actually experienced and practitioners can see how certain modes fit certain skills.

Body and mind

Working through the different modes of learning involves a complex synthesis of physical and perceptual systems and responses. For instance, observation and copying of behaviour or a particular skill may involve complicated processing so that the eventual execution replicates the example. Mental and emotional aspects can be involved. The child may want to be like the person he is watching and copying, and therefore there is a strong motivation. Emulation of adults, peers and professional sportsmen and women can play a large part in the emotional, attitudinal and motivational aspects of

learning, even when the child is very young. Furthermore, not being successful in front of other children and negative peer pressure can have long-term detrimental results on the confidence and self-esteem of the child.

Consolidating learning: does practice make perfect?

It is important to reconsider how children learn physical skills through the three-part learning process – acquisition, development and consolidation. The process takes time; it is fortunate that young children enjoy repetition and revisiting skills, and practitioners should exploit this factor.

The general competence of the child improves as each separate skill goes through the sequence of initial acquisition, development, enhancement and eventual consolidation. When one particular skill becomes sound and eventually almost automatic and internalized, the child can cope with a new, more complex skill. As long as the child is not over-challenged, *practice does indeed make sound, if not perfect*. Practical advice for practitioners can be to remember these key words: time (to explore and play); repetition; success; enjoyment; praise; and more time (to show off achievement).

The older child (six years plus) will be exploring more complex and refined movement patterns, for instance, striking a small ball with a hockey stick, or shooting a ball at a mini-netball goal. In these linked sequences of movements there is a requirement for motor planning: in other words, a conscious thought

and ordering behind the movements. The older child may actually run through a sort of 'mental rehearsal' of the sequence of actions, thinking about the beginning, middle and end phases of the movement pattern, or its 'preparation, action and recovery' (Macintyre 2001, p. 77). An adult would use this conscious movement planning, sometimes spending too much time planning to the detriment of the resultant action.

A very important aspect of mastering a skill or linked series of skills is the element of repetition making the movement pattern habitual. When a movement pattern becomes habitual the skill has become second nature, internalized and never forgotten: the particular motor strings, movement patterns and skills execution have become ingrained in 'muscle memory'. Once the child 'knows' how to skip, or to run up stairs, he will not lose this skill. This is the type of learning (or 'knowing') that Foster (1976) describes in the title to her book on movement education, *Knowing in my bones*. Children take great pleasure in this knowing: they say, 'I know how to swim ...' or 'I can do that ...!'

The learning spiral

The process of physical skill learning can be visualized as a spiral. The three-part learning process (acquisition, development and consolidation of skill) can be expanded to explain more complex forms of physical learning. The learning can be seen to take the form of an upward spiral as further, new

explorations build upon initial learning. As skills are practised or revisited, they become more established and efficient.

If, for example, the infant wishes to build a tower of blocks, he will place the first block down on the floor, then he will attempt to place the second block on top of the first. Depending upon his fine motor dexterity and his block-management skills (and also perhaps on chance), the attempt may be fairly successful and the second block fairly square with the first, so he might be able to balance the third and fourth blocks. It would be no good at all for an adult to tell the child how to do this placing and management: the child needs to experience it and *do* it. As he does so, he is experiencing feedback from the weight, the lifting and management of the block, and he is using visual skill. He knows and can see when he is successful. He repeats his game, repeating the cycle of events, internalizes the learning and enjoys his successful result.

When he tries a subsequent endeavour (perhaps a higher tower), he is already beginning from a new, higher, more informed starting point in his learning. He never goes back to the level of his very first attempt, because he has actually experienced the physical learning. His learning is not a cyclical loop, but an improving, upward spiral. A visualization of this spiral can be seen in Figure 4.1.

This spiral echoes the three-part process of learning (acquisition, development and con-solidation). The child tries out a new skill; he experiments and explores the skill; he considers his achievement and tries a new exploration from an

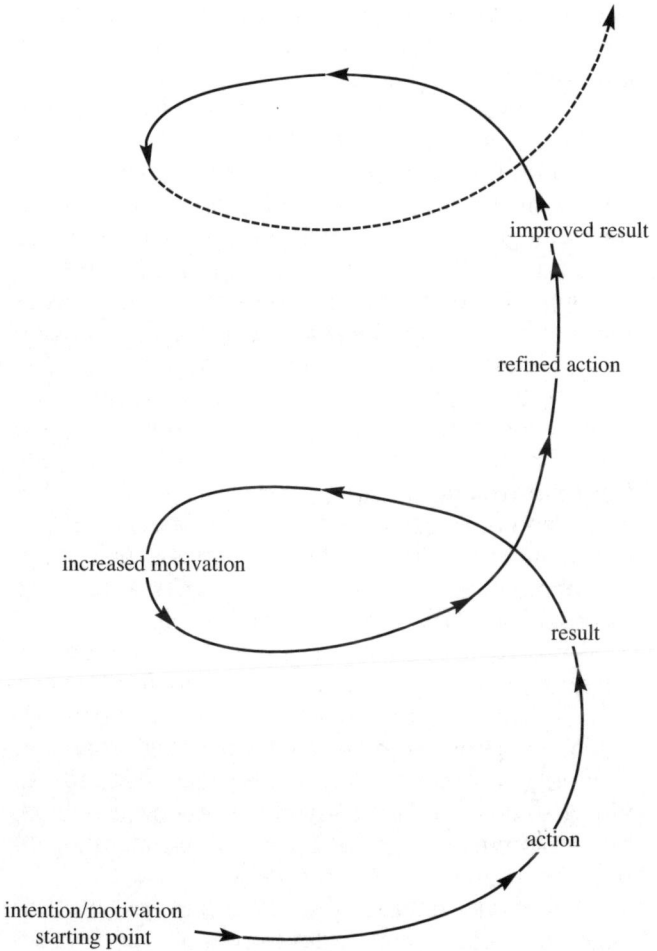

Figure 4.1   The learning spiral

improved baseline of ability. All forms of physical endeavour, physical skill acquisition, skill practice and refinement follow the process through the spiral of learning.

As the child develops and explores more specific skills in Key Stage One and Two, he will carry out more actual planning of movement and more judgemental evaluation (of his own work and that of others). The younger child is more involved in exploring, experimenting, finding success and enjoyment in achievement as he experiences the spiral. Successful execution breeds desire for further exploration and experimentation. Enjoyment of the endeavour, together with praise and encouragement from adults, fuel further explorations. The spiral can be said to be one of success.

However, the reverse application is also true: failed attempts are not enjoyable and are less likely to be repeated. A spiral of failure, together with the resultant lack of self-esteem and confidence, can result where the child may give up attempting to master new skills.

It can be seen that the setting of *appropriate* challenges is of vital importance. The supportive structural skill-scaffolding must be sound so that he can make the next step. As he does so, the child can be encouraged to develop positive attitudes such as perseverance and application. In the real world, many attempts at skill mastery are going to result in initial failure; the young child needs encouragement and validation that his trial-and-error attempts are *in themselves* of value.

Observing children in action

Knowledge of the ways in which children learn can support the development of practitioners' observation skills. Expertise in planning, selection of activities, guidance and teaching depends upon careful observation of children. It takes time to develop this educated eye. The practitioner has to judge the skills, strengths and difficulties of each child in order to plan the next learning step. The casual observer of children's play does not see with the teacher's eye.

It can be helpful to think of the aesthetics of a movement – how it looks, because ragged, untidy, over-exaggerated movement usually indicates an immature movement pattern. Obviously, the success of the end result or product also indicates skill (or lack of it). The practitioner can help the child by considering his difficulties. Practitioners should also look at body posture and at timing. Immature movement patterns take great effort, they are not smooth and there are extraneous, unnecessary movements: for example, a five-year-old cutting out may use the scissors in a jerky fashion and he may have his tongue in the corner of his mouth. Immature football skills may show in an overlong run up with arms waving, resulting in over-kicking or missing of the ball. Skilled performance is smooth, with perfect timing and seems effortless.

Help with movement observation, recording and 'assessment'

The following aspects are based upon developmental principles and how children actually learn.

78

How Children Learn in the Physical Domain

These points can provide a basic framework for observation and will be helpful when recording and assessing outcomes: age of the subject (developmental level, general health for age) is the activity new or familiar? posture: natural good body tension or not? phases: preparation, execution, recovery; timing of movements: extremes – very slowly, very quickly, or smooth flow? effective use of body part or parts (isolations); extraneous movements: too much effort, wobbling, arm movement?; aesthetics of the movement: purity of line or ragged and untidy?; and attitudes manifested: confidence, anxiety, pleasure, frustration …?

These elements can help practitioners make judgements about the activity they are watching and enable them to consider how to help particular children, by, for example, adapting the task or the equipment or the speed factors involved. It is good practice to discuss observations with colleagues, as verbalizing movement is part of movement analysis. Discussion can aid decisions as to planning effective strategies for progress. Sometimes, repeated attempts at the same game or skill can lead to success for the child; in other circumstances, a practitioner may engage the child with a simplified version of the endeavour; in yet other instances, the child may be helped by instruction and manipulation; or in certain cases, a fresh game may be deemed appropriate.

In the realms of physical play and physical education, action and achievements occur at speed and in a moment of time. This temporal nature of the activities means that effective written recording

of observations is difficult. One effective, realistic method is to carry a small notebook for quick comments or drawings. It has to be said, however, that most effective recording of achievement takes place in the practitioner's head. In many cases this special knowledge is adequate: the practitioner makes an on-the-spot assessment of the achievement or difficulties and is able to plan the next learning task.

While it is unrealistic to record every single aspect of physical learning for each child, it is good practice to record major learning steps and any problems which occur. A working checklist, covering the gross and fine motor skills and movement vocabulary for a particular unit, can be a useful strategy as a basis for producing a working profile for each child. A useful exercise to train the practitioner's eye can be to focus on and to track, one child in a particular session (Sharman *et al.* 2000).

Early years practitioners continually watch, consider and assess learning and achievement; these factors are intrinsic elements of pedagogy. Understanding how children learn can enable practitioners to facilitate learning. It is important to use appropriate teaching methods which reflect the three-part process of skill learning and the endeavour–success–enjoyment spiral and which utilize action, play, exploration, repetition and praise.

5

Good Practice, Safe Practice: Supporting and Facilitating Physical Learning

It has been demonstrated that experiential learning encompasses all aspects of what could be called psychophysical development, and that this learning involves the 'whole child'. This early learning is physical learning; everything the child does is part of this physical and sensory education and it is important that the child develops independence and autonomy as his confidence grows. Alongside the development of physical competence and the general health benefits of active engagement, aspects of emotional, personal, cognitive and social development are also established and enhanced. The work of the practitioner supports and affects all these aspects of development.

The healthy child

The physical education of the young child should always help him to understand about his body, how to keep active and healthy and why these things are important. The very young child can be encouraged to eat a healthy diet, his efforts at play-exercise praised and his emotions tempered. Habits of a

lifetime are forged in infancy. Unfortunately, for many children these aspects are not encouraged, and parental and sibling role models are not exemplars of healthy living. Obesity is on the increase, with 'ten per cent of children beginning primary school classified as obese' (Pritchard 2003, p. 24). 'Junk food' is what many children are fed, and physical games and play opportunities can be limited by environmental and safety factors.

Good practice, good health

Good practice in nurseries and infant schools should therefore include daily action sessions where the group or class come together to do some enjoyable, suitable physical activities. Songs and rhymes with actions can be extended into simple stretches to the sky and curls to the floor plus short sections of jogging and bouncing on toes. There should be time to talk about how the children feel when they have been active, about hygiene and about foods they like and foods which are good for them. It is very important that practitioners explain to the children why health and fitness issues are important. These aspects are highlighted in the Early Learning Goals for health and bodily awareness, in *Curriculum Guidance for the Foundation Stage* (QCA/DfEE 2000, pp. 110, 111).

Children enjoy hands-on opportunities for preparing, making, baking and eating appropriate foods (fruit salads, for example), accompanied by talking and sharing. This kind of activity goes beyond the fine and gross motor skill learning and

application advantages, reaching into social learning. It can also be a good opportunity for parents to come in, to help and to share in the learning.

Being safe

Understanding about good health also encompasses safety aspects, management of risk, challenge, autonomy and independence and knowing how to keep oneself safe.

Some children are extremely timid, while others show no fear. The 'outside classroom' can be the domain where these issues come to the fore, as can the hall for P.E. sessions and some classroom areas. In the outside classroom the children are able to play and explore a range of outdoor equipment. Nursery children can 'experiment with the 'big behaviors' (*sic*) such as shouting, running, climbing and jumping' (Rivkin 2000, p. 1). Older children can experiment like this during play times and lunch breaks as well.

Children need to learn simple rules about play and behaviour, so that safe practice becomes a part of each activity.

Older children also need to be reminded of the rules for appropriate play outside. Children need to understand when shouting is not acceptable and when rough-and-tumble play becomes inappropriate. The playground should be a place where the principles of safe practice are exemplified. Many schools and nurseries have a special, resilient, shock-absorbent surface built under climbing equipment. The climbing equipment can be fixed, but moveable,

Cameo

At Rainbow Nursery, children are taught that the mini-climbing frame is only used when an adult is standing by it and that only four people can use the climbing frame at once. The climbing frame is not used every day. The children learn that they can only ride wheeled vehicles on a particular part of the area and that balls should not be sent across where other people are playing. They do not play on the grassy slope if it has been raining and the ground is slippery.

add-on equipment can be more challenging and offer more creative challenge to children because resources can be adapted to suit the children's play ideas (Bilton 1998, p. 31). Improving playgrounds and making them exciting, stimulating places, with areas for quiet play as well as spaces and equipment for active play, can improve behaviour and social interaction and reduce aggression (Rivkin 2000). It is good practice to carry out and record a risk assessment chart for the outdoor classroom and the playground, with diagrams of the equipment, noting all the safety procedures and requirements in place and any special needs of the children. This should be changed and updated each half term, or as circumstances demand.

Appropriate behaviour should be praised by practitioners and this should reinforce this aspect of

learning. In the physical domain, appropriate behaviour is safe behaviour. Practitioners should also talk to the children to explain about behaviours which are inappropriate and unsafe: the child needs to acquire knowledge and understanding about safety aspects by direct instruction as well as from praise. This type of learning should not be open to chance or 'caught'; it should be taught. Where children are working in a self-directed environment, as in a High Scope system, for example, this type of learning is of paramount importance. The young child should begin to understand safety aspects and to develop his safety repertoire alongside his movement repertoire.

Management strategies I

Practitioners need to consider how differing learning challenges will be presented to children. Planning for safety should become second nature for practitioners and be embedded within all teaching and management strategies. *Good practice is safe practice*. Practitioners will develop a repertoire of teaching styles and management strategies which can be employed to suit particular circumstances and which match with the developmental stages of the children.

In early years practice, the practitioner is encouraging and supporting learning (as is the parent in the first instance) rather than directly teaching. However, facilitating, supporting, guiding and engineering of the environment and resources are all aspects of pedagogy which can be placed under the umbrella term of 'teaching'.

Physical Development in the Early Years

The main teaching styles which the early years practitioner uses are: facilitative; problem-setting; and directional or didactic. The practitioner using the *facilitative* teaching style would be concerned with providing an appropriate, stimulating environment. The environment and the resources should be set up to encourage the child to explore particular motor skills and sensory elements. Initially, the child may engage in free play activity. The practitioner's role is complex. She needs to utilize guidance and feedback, ask pertinent questions and have good observation skills. She will assess achievements and difficulties and make evaluative judgements which can be built into future planning. The environment could be an area of the room for a group playdough activity, the hall for a large apparatus session, the outdoor classroom or a part of the garden area.

The *problem-setting* teaching style is based upon the setting of open-ended challenges and tasks and involves the child in problem-solving. The practitioner has a focused aim behind this style. The challenges and tasks must match the maturity and developmental level of the child yet, at the same time, extend his learning. The child should 'be introduced to new learning situations and ... be given the opportunity to restructure existing knowledge and transfer inherent skills ... to new situations and problems in order to find solutions' (Moyles 1996, p. 32).

This style of teaching can be seen as an extension of facilitative teaching, as the environment is set up in close relation to the skills

to be explored. There will be learning objectives which could be wide (using a Year One gymnastic activity session example: 'To explore ways of travelling on feet') or quite closed (same example: 'To learn resilient, squashy landings'). The practitioner will set particular tasks or problems: 'Can you show me a really quiet way of travelling on your feet?' (an open task) or, 'Let me see everyone tucked up into a small ball' (a more closed task). Table 5.1 shows an example of this teaching style.

The *directional or didactic* teaching style can be said to be command- or instruction-based. There is an implication that there is a correct (and safe) way of doing something and that the practitioner is saying, 'Do this now ...' and/or 'Do it like this ...'.

Class: Year One	
Environment: Hall, low-level apparatus.	
Equipment, resources	**Skills to be exercised**
The floor	Travelling, spatial awareness
Benches	Balance, travelling along
Mats	Springs, jumps, 'squashy' landings
Hoops	Agility, footwork, step patterns
Problem/tasks:	
'Can you show me some interesting ways of travelling on hands and feet?' 'Can you jump from the bench and land softly, bending knees?'	
NC Gymnastic activities: 8 a and b.	

Table 5.1   Problem-setting teaching style: examples of equipment, skills and problems/tasks set

There may also be practical demonstration as the child is directed and given verbal instructions, for example, on how to hold a bat correctly. Directional teaching can be used in conjunction with other styles of teaching and the practitioner may use a mix, moving from one style to another from one minute to the next.

Management strategies II

Practitioners need to know that they can plan to manage the children and the learning opportunities effectively and safely. The main aspects for consideration are: the environment (space, resources, people, equipment); the learning objectives ('What do I want the children to explore/learn?'); time allocation (setting time for experimentation and tidying up); techniques for observation and assessment ('Have they learned anything?'); and control mechanisms (voice, percussion instrument, songs, whistle for outdoors).

Organizational issues involve the changing of the children into safe, appropriate clothing or kit and arranging which adults supervise the gathering and setting out of equipment. Lining up and travelling to the work area are also safety issues, and commands and strategies should be taught to the children to help. Using a song or a chant for lining up can be an enjoyable way to teach listen, respond and react skills and to train the children in safe procedures. These strategies are effective control mechanisms which can be built into the activities so that responding to a sound, whistle or rhyme is an

enjoyable part of the game. How much initiative and independence is shown by each child regarding changing, setting up and carrying equipment will be directed by the practitioner who should strive to encourage autonomy, but also be realistic. Taking time to go over procedures and practices will pay off as the children learn the systems and routines. Practitioners should go over the procedures and rules for stopping, listening and carrying equipment at the beginning of every session.

The timing of sessions is important and depends upon the learning objectives set by the practitioner, the environment and resources and the interest and motivation of the children. A balance of time for exploration, instruction, guidance and fresh exploration follows the principles of the process of physical learning. Time must be given for talk, praise and for showing and sharing achievement. Judgement of pace and timing within a session does develop with experience.

Practical sessions should be frequent: daily if possible. In primary schools, sessions are often 30 minutes long (including changing times), but it is difficult to set constraints and expectations. Over-long sessions (one hour) which occur once or twice a week are not as valuable as several shorter sessions in terms of fitness and learning potential.

Planning and content

No matter which learning modes are to be covered or which teaching styles the practitioner is going to use, it is vital that the established skill base of the child is

visited before new learning is expected. The learning objectives should always build upon what the child already knows and is confident about. The practitioner must base subsequent learning steps upon the observations she has made, any assessments recorded and discussion with colleagues. The actual content of units of work and individual session plans should be based upon the skills and movement vocabulary that the child is to experience and should match up to expected levels of physical development and maturity. Questions the practitioner must ask herself include: 'What can the child do now, what skills/knowledge does he possess?', and 'What do I want him to learn/explore next, and which skills are involved?' Following the child's experimentation and engagement, the practitioner should reflect and carry out assessment based upon her observations and ask herself: 'Has the child developed new skills, new competence: *has learning taken place*?'

Effective planning is a progressive, cyclical process. Practitioners have to be responsive, but also proactive and able to adapt, as the practical outcomes may not be as expected. It is important that practitioners plan experiences bearing in mind the three-part process of physical skill learning (acquisition, development and consolidation).

Sessions should always contain the following elements: warming up and channelling body and mind; revisiting established skills and movement vocabulary; introduction of new skills and movement vocabulary; tasks for experimentation and exploration; and time for praise, questioning, showing and sharing achievement, coming together and discussion.

These elements apply universally, whether the session is a class dance session in the hall, a games session outside or for a small group activity such as paper weaving.

Content

The framework content of early years curricula in nurseries and schools is based upon the *Curriculum Guidance for the Foundation Stage* (QCA/DfEE 2000), *The National Curriculum* (1999) and the QCA *Scheme of Work* for PE (QCA 2000). Nevertheless, it must be stressed that physical learning occurs across the whole curriculum.

In the main, physical learning will come under the headings of 'Gross and fine motor skill activities', 'Sensory activities' and 'Spatial awareness'. It is important that children gain competence and confidence in the management of self, space and control (*Foundation Stage Profile Handbook*, QCA/DfES 2003, p. 51). The children should be acquiring and developing a range of skills and a wide movement vocabulary. At the same time, they should be developing and exercising appropriate attitudes, concepts and dispositions.

In Key Stages One and Two, the skills and movement content is separated out and classified as games, gymnastic and dance activities. These activities should take place in indoor and outdoor environments. Swimming and water safety, athletic activities and outdoor and adventurous activities are listed in Key Stage Two, but certain aspects of these activities may be covered earlier in some settings and circumstances.

Content of games activity sessions

Games activity sessions should provide opportunities for practice of relevant skills, exploration of equipment, and management of self and space. A games session should have sections for free play, for individual and paired tasks (if appropriate) and for actual skills teaching (guided play). An example of an actual games session plan for a Nursery/Reception class is shown in Table 5.2.

The basic games-based skills are travelling, sending, receiving and directing equipment, which leads into dodging, marking, catching, throwing and shooting skills. In order to aid the acquisition and development of these skills, it is necessary for practitioners to take apart each skill and to slow down the activity. Pre-catching work should contain rolling and bouncing, both of which slow down the pathway of the ball and give time for the motor string of catching to transmit through to small hands. Targets and goals should be accessible for small children. The skills can be practised in shuttle drills or races and appropriate mini-games. The child should strive to better his own scores in individual tasks before he is asked to take part in larger scale competitive mini-games.

Content of movement sessions (gymnastic and dance activities)

At first, body management skills and movement vocabulary do not need to be subdivided into those used in gymnastic activities and those used in dance. The child needs to develop a repertoire of movement

skills which aid body control, balance, space and weight management, leading to confident overall body management. He will enjoy adding to this repertoire and being creative with his skills, making simple movement patterns and repeating them. He may transfer sequences of travelling, balancing, held shapes, leaping and landing skills onto apparatus in gymnastic activities. He will link travelling ideas such as darting, twisting, turning movements with stillness, held shape and balance skills to make creative patterns in dance sessions.

A basic *vocabulary of movement* is made up of locomotive or travelling skills and space management activities. The toddler will develop skills in this basic vocabulary as soon as he begins to walk and travel in space. In sessions at school, the child will extend and add to his movement repertoire, learning to speak in movement, using his own creative ideas. He may roll, twist, crumple and slither without knowing the spoken words. However, his spoken vocabulary develops alongside his movement vocabulary, as he names body parts and learns new movement words.

The use of appropriate music can aid enjoyment and develop rhythmic responses and timing skills. The child should be given opportunities to explore levels and direction and simple dynamics should be covered, such as strong shapes, jagged shapes, light tiptoeing and heavy stamping (dynamics means *how* a movement is carried out, the mood or quality of a movement). Music can dictate the dynamic quality of movements, and practitioners can exploit percussion instruments for this. The cameo which follows shows part of a Year Three dance session.

Physical Development in the Early Years

Date: May 2003	Class: Nursery/RCN
Timing: 40 minutes	OUTDOORS

Physical Development:
Outdoor Games Activities – playground, grass
Early Learning Goals:	Move with control and co-ordination. Show awareness of space, of themselves and others. Use range of small and large equipment.
Skills and movement vocabulary:
Bubble space – stretch, bend, tuck, shake-out (non-locomotor). Travelling – walk, jog, hop, springs, little jumps (locomotor). Manipulative – sending, trapping, receiving, following, tracking.
Resources:	Big and small balls, foam balls, plastic bats, bean bags, ropes, hoops, marker cones.
Warm-up:	Adults put out boxes of equip. Remind children of rules for safe work. Shake-out, loosener on spot. Bubble space, stretches, bends, reaches, arm swings, springs, jumps, jog. Walk around section of playgd, jog, STOP, shake body part, repeat. 'Are we feeling warm?'
Development:	Show and talk thru' equip, re-cap safe work. 'What could we do with this?' Children choose equip: BLUE group: balls, bean bags, hoops RED group: ropes, hoops, bean bags GREEN group: foam balls, plastic bats, hoops. One adult per group.
Explore and experiment:	Praise, look, talk. Set tasks for individuals. Change groups and rotate after 8 mins approx. Explore new equip.
Show and share:	Watch, praise, try out.
Conclusion:	Children put equip back into correct boxes.
Cool-down:	Stretch, swing arms, jog, reach. 'Simon Says': hands on head, hands on shoulders, bounce shoulders. Praise.
Line up, stand tall, walk inside. Dressing. Helpers move boxes.

Table 5.2   A Foundation Stage session plan

Cameo: Class 3W Dance. Theme: The Sea

Resources and stimuli: tambourine and rain-maker, played by the teacher; whooshing sea sounds made by the children

The tambourine was shaken and beaten to be the stimulus for different sea creatures, working with the children's suggestions; the rainmaker suggested the advance and retreat of the waves. The children made additional sea sounds if they wished.

The children have reached the development stage of the lesson, having explored travelling ideas from waves and sea creatures and non-locomotor ideas such as waving sea weed and shells opening and snapping shut.

Ian's group of four children are working on a pattern which uses scuttling crabs, floating jellyfish and a large whale swimming. The dynamic qualities of this group's work show rapid, sharp, low movements and soft, waving, undulating travelling ideas.

Sarah's group is working on ideas from a high-stepping sea horse, waves crashing and whirlpools swirling down. They are trying out a formation idea of two children facing the other two and travelling in and out, waves crashing as they meet. Their ideas show soft and fierce dynamics, high and low levels and advancing, crashing and retreating travelling.

> *All of the groups are talking, trying out ideas and linking three or four elements in their dance.*

This cameo shows some good practice in a creative dance session. There is a mix of ideas for movement; the children's own ideas, those suggested by the teacher and those suggested by the instruments. The teacher has been able to evoke the waves, the undersea world and the creatures therein. This has really stimulated and excited the children into experimentation. When they have composed their short patterns the groups will show and share the work in progress. This will allow time for comments and suggestions from the other children, as well as praise from the teacher.

When planning for gymnastic and dance activities, practitioners should write a list of movement vocabulary to be explored for each lesson plan. This is good practice which really pays off, as the practitioner has to be very clear about the movement content of the session.

Content for developing manipulative skills and sensory awareness

Manipulative, fine motor skills and sensory aware-ness will also be explored across the curriculum. There should be opportunities for art and craft, making, designing, and construction activities. Sand and water play activities, involving pouring,

estimating, measuring and weighing, allow the child to experience science and mathematics and to develop significant language.

'Small world' play equipment enables the child to enact scenarios from real life and to manipulate an environment. Practical, creative music sessions develop manipulative skills and exercise listening skills. Puzzle play equipment and maths games exercise the brain as well as the fingers. Important attitudes such as perseverance, sharing and waiting for turns are also being developed, and in all of these examples both process and product are significant. It is very important to use hands-on methods of learning like these throughout the primary school.

The learning journey and the pedagogic process

The child is at the heart of the pedagogic process. His age, maturity, developmental level, aptitudes and interests provide the starting point for the practitioner, who embarks upon the organic, complicated process of observing, planning, allowing for learning, reviewing and reflecting. Theory, knowledge, practice and experience come together as the practitioner sifts, selects, enacts and reacts to the children and their requirements. This complexity of the process of practice is reflected in the Key Statements of the SPEEL Report Framework for Effective Pedagogy (Moyles *et al.* 2002, pp. 51–6) and practitioners' knowledge of children's physical development is stressed in particular:

Effective practitioners have knowledge and understanding of ...

2. *all aspects of child development, including theories of, and approaches to, learning...*
3. *how to combine and apply pedagogic knowledge and understanding so that teaching and learning experiences are congruent with children's development ...*
4. *multi-sensory learning and teaching approaches for young children ...*
14. *safety issues and application to practice ...*

This process of planning, teaching and reflecting is in fact a spiral process, like the learning spiral which the children experience, and leads to an enhanced beginning, as the practitioner builds upon what has been seen and learnt. Thus, both the child and the practitioner are learning.

The learning journey

Real learning is active, physical learning which is holistic in nature and affects the whole person. Physical development, sensory awareness and sense of self depend upon appropriate experiential learning and engagement. Experiences in the early years mould the future adult, and a healthy, contented body and mind make a well-balanced person who will be able to cope with the rigours of life.

The human child takes a remarkable journey, from birth and relative dependence upon others, through his early years, acquiring body mastery and sensory awareness, coping with a widening world,

social and emotional elements and with varying educational settings. The journey takes the child past several milestones of development, achievement and independence as he widens his repertoire of physical, mental, emotional and social skills. Early years practitioners have a unique and privileged role as they accompany each child on this learning journey.

Becoming a sensitive and effective early years practitioner is also a unique journey. It is a journey which is physical and ongoing, as the learning never stops and each new child teaches and changes his educators. Practice and pedagogy are challenged every day by the children, by their excitement, actions and reactions.

The overall development of the child and his success in the education system is affected for ever by the early years practitioners he encounters. He cannot complete his physical and sensory development journey without effective help from these practitioners. Physical and mental well-being, self-esteem and confidence are all affected by early experiences. Those of us who are fortunate enough to be part of this exciting process of early childhood education know both the importance of this special learning journey and that we are indeed privileged to be co-travellers.

References

Aslin, R. (1981) 'Development of smooth pursuit in human infants', in Fisher, D., Monty, R. and Senders, J. (eds) *Eye Movements: Cognition and Visual Perception*. Hillsdale, NJ: Erlbaum.

Barber, P. and Legge, D. (1976) *Perception and Information*. London: Methuen.

Bee, H. (1995) *The Growing Child*. London: Harper Collins.

Bilton, H. (1998) *Outdoor Play in the Early Years*. London: David Fulton.

Buschner, C. (1994) *Teaching Children Movement Concepts and Skills*. Leeds: Human Kinetics.

Bruner, J. (1983) *Child's Talk*. New York: Norton.

Bruner, J., Olver, R. and Greenfield, P. (1966) *Studies in Cognitive Growth*. New York: John Wiley.

Cocks, N. (1992) *Skipping Not Tripping*. Simon and Schuster, London

Cratty, B. (1986) *Perceptual and Motor Development in Infants and Young Children*. London: Prentice Hall.

Curtis, A. and O'Hagan, M. (2003) *Care and Education in Early Childhood*. London, Routledge Falmer.

David, T. (1999) *Young Children Learning*. London: Paul Chapman.

Dennison, P. and Dennison, G. (1994) *Brain Gym Teacher's Edition*. Ventura: Edu-kinesthetics, Inc.

DfEE (1999) *The National Curriculum, Key Stages 1 and 2*. London: DfEE, QCA.

Doherty, J. and Bailey, R. (2003) *Supporting Physical*

References

Development and Physical Education in the Early Years. Buckingham: Open University Press.

Donaldson, M. (1978) *Children's Minds.* Glasgow: Fontana, Collins.

Foster, R. (1976) *Knowing in My Bones.* London: A. and C. Black.

Gallahue, D. and Ozmun, J. (1998) *Understanding Motor Development.* Boston, MA: McGraw Hill.

Harris, M. and Butterworth, G. (2002) *Developmental Psychology.* Hove: Psychology Press Ltd.

Keenan, T. (2002) *An Introduction to Child Development.* London: Sage Publications.

Kohlberg, L. (1966) 'A cognitive developmental analysis of children's sex role concepts and attitudes', in E. Maccaby (ed.) *The Development of Sex Differences.* Stanford, CA: Stanford University Press.

Laban, R., revised by Ullmann, L. (1988) *Modern Educational Dance.* Plymouth: Northcote House Publishers.

Macintyre, C. (2000) *Dyspraxia in the Early Years.* London: David Fulton.

— (2001) *Enhancing Learning Through Play.* London: David Fulton.

Maude, P. (2001) *Physical Children, Active Teaching.* Buckingham: Open University Press.

Moyles, J. (1996) *Just Playing?* Buckingham: Open University Press.

Moyles, J., Adams, S. and Musgrave, A. (2002) *Study of Pedagogical Effectiveness in Early Learning*, DfES Research Report RR 363. London: DfES.

Pritchard, A. (2003) 'Time for action', *Nursery World*, April 2003.

QCA (2000) *Scheme of Work, Physical Education, Key Stages One and Two.* London: QCA.

QCA/DfEE (2000) *Curriculum Guidance for the Foundation Stage.* London: QCA.

Physical Development in the Early Years

QCA/DfES (2003) *Foundation Stage Profile Handbook*. London: QCA, DfES.

Parten, M. (1933) 'Social play amongst pre-school children', *Journal of Abnormal and Social Psychology*, 28.

Piaget, J. (1971) *Science of Education and the Psychology of the Child*. London: Longman.

Ripley, K., Daines B., and Barrett, J. (1998) *Dyspraxia, A Guide for Teachers and Parents*. London: David Fulton.

Rivkin, M. (2000) 'Outdoor experiences for young children', *ERIC Clearinghouse on Rural Education and Small Schools*, December 2000.

Rosenbaum, D. (1991) *Human Motor Control*. London: Academic Press Ltd.

Seefeldt, (1984) in Poest, C., Williams, J. Witt, D., and Atwood, M. (1990) 'Challenge me to move: large muscle development in young children', *Young Children*, July 1990.

Sharman, C., Cross, W. and Vennis, D. (2000) *Observing Children*. London: Cassell.

Sherbourne, V. (1993) *Developmental Movement for Children: Main Stream, Special Needs and Pre-school*. Cambridge: Cambridge University Press.

Sheridan, M. (1995) *From Birth to Five Years, Children's Developmental Progress*. London: Routledge.

Smith, P., Cowie, H. and Blades, M. (2003) *Understanding Children's Development*. Oxford: Blackwell.

Thelen, E. (1995) 'Motor development: a new synthesis', *American Psychologist Journal*, Vol. 50, Feb. 1995.

Vygotsky, L. (1978) *Mind in Society*. Cambridge, MA: Harvard.

Wittgenstein, L. (1991) *Philosophical Investigations*. Oxford: Basil Blackwell.

Wood, D., Bruner, J. and Ross, G. (1976) 'The role of tutoring in problem-solving', *Journal of Child Psychology and Psychiatry*, Vol. 17.

Woodfield, L. (1992) Research project leading to unpublished M.Ed. Dissertation, University of Exeter.